"Grief is often compounded by the complex decisions and questions one faces in the aftermath of loss. The bereaved can look to *Seriously, God?* as a tool, a resource, and most importantly, a companion as they navigate the messy struggle of the spirituality of suffering."

Jeannie Ewing
Author of *From Grief to Grace*

"This book brims with hope and inspiration for a world desperately lacking both. These authors and parish leaders dive into life's toughest questions with a down-to-earth writing style that makes deep mysteries accessible to anyone. Whether you're away from God or in love with him, if you're on the mountaintop or in the valley, this book will meet you where you are and inspire you with images and stories that stick. More, please!"

Chris Stefanick
Founder and president of Real Life Catholic

"What you'll find in White and Corcoran's book is an honest and direct reflection on the age-old challenge of reconciling two seemingly opposed realties: faith in an all-powerful, all-loving God, and living in a world where suffering and sadness prevail all too often. A worthwhile read for those wrestling with this paradox."

Curtis Martin
Founder of FOCUS

"Have you ever questioned God? I know I have many times and I have not always been satisfied with the answers or seeming lack thereof. In *Seriously, God?*, Fr. Michael White and Tom Corcoran dive deep into examining the whys we all ask in hard times, and they remind us that our stories are still being written with only God knowing how they end. This book will challenge you to seek the Lord in every joyful or sorrow-filled chapter of your beautiful life."

Mary Lenaburg
Author of *Be Brave in the Scared*

SERIOUSLY,

Making Sense of Life Not Making Sense

GOD?

Michael White
and Tom Corcoran

AVE MARIA PRESS AVE Notre Dame, Indiana

Founded in 1865, Ave Maria Press is a ministry of the United States Province of Holy
Cross.

www.avemariapress.com

Paperback: ISBN-13 978-1-64680-084-1

E-book: ISBN-13 978-1-64680-085-8

Special Edition product number: 30007

Cover image © Artem Beliaikin on Unsplash.

Cover and text design by Andy Wagoner.

Printed and bound in the United States of America.

Library of Congress Cataloging-in-Publication Data
Names: White, Michael, 1958- author. | Corcoran, Tom, author.
Title: Seriously, God? : making sense of life not making sense / Michael
    White and Tom Corcoran.
Description: Notre Dame, IN : Ave Maria Press, [2021] | Summary: "The
    authors of this book encourage open conversations about the genuine
    doubts, confusion, and seemingly contradictory assertions about the
    nature of God that often arise out of intense human suffering. They
    explore feeling denied and even betrayed by God, struggling to
    understand why God allows bad things to happen all around us"-- Provided
    by publisher.
Identifiers: LCCN 2021019029 | ISBN 9781646800841 (paperback) | ISBN
    9781646800841 (ebook)
Subjects: LCSH: Suffering--Religious aspects--Christianity.
Classification: LCC BV4909 .W488 2021 | DDC 248.8/6--dc23
LC record available at https://lccn.loc.gov/2021019029

TO TOM GRADY,
who believed in us
(when others didn't)

CONTENTS

Preface

Tom: The day was perfect. Everything at church was going well; we were enjoying a rare absence of challenges. Rarer still, when I got home, all was at peace in my house full of kids. Rarest of all, for a February day in Baltimore, the sun was shining and the temperature had reached 65 degrees. So, the only thing on my mind was getting out in the fresh air as soon as possible and going for a run.

Once home, I quickly changed clothes. Then I grabbed my phone and put in my earbuds so I could listen to music. I have two playlists—one sacred, which contains current Christian music; the other secular, with rock and classic rock from Van Halen, Led Zeppelin, and U2. I don't remember which list I chose, but I know I turned the volume all the way up. I was excited for the run.

At the front door, my two-year-old daughter Lydia waved and blew me a kiss. Lydia's a charmer, and she gets me every time. I slowed down just long enough to pat her on the head and then took off across the front yard and down the street.

The run was everything I wanted it to be. Some days you run, and it's all work. Other times you run, and it's pure joy. This run was pure joy, and I was feeling good about life. Until I got back home.

My wife, Mia, was standing at the door with a look of what I can only describe as utter horror. "What's wrong?" I asked. "Lydia," she barely managed to say. "What's happened?" "I don't know. We're not sure. A couple was driving down Old Harford Road and Lydia was in the middle of the street. They stopped and rescued her, learned from neighbors where she lives, and brought her back."

Old Harford is about fifty yards from my house. It is a very busy thoroughfare, especially at that time of day, when drivers seem more than usually willing to ignore the speed limit.

Mia continued through her tears, "Apparently Lydia wanted to run with you and followed you down the street, but when she got to the intersection, she became confused and disoriented." Neither of us said what we couldn't stop thinking: Lydia could have been killed. We had nearly lost our precious daughter.

I was shaken by what had happened. It took some soul searching to try to fill in the details and put the story together. Eventually I began to realize that my irresponsibility and self-absorption had nearly led to my daughter's death. I was so focused on getting outside and going for a run that I just took off, completely unmindful of her. Music blasting in my ears ensured I did not hear her calls to join me. I guess I thought she would stay at the house. I suppose I assumed the other kids were watching her. But truth be told, I wasn't really thinking about anything but myself.

I experienced a mix of two conflicting emotions: enormous gratitude that God had spared my daughter and crushing guilt at the thought of a terrible tragedy. Later that night came a third emotion—confusion. God had spared my child. There was no doubt in my mind that he had protected her, but then I couldn't help but think of Tom and Pam.

Tom and Pam are two of the most generous people we know. They are generous in every sense of the word—with their time, their money, their spirit. They are generous listeners and wonderful hosts. They are especially generous in their service to the Church. Tom and Pam had lost their beloved son Christopher, in a car accident in his junior year in high school, at the hands of a drunk driver. We couldn't help but think that if God could have spared them the tragedy of losing their son, why didn't he?

At the time, we were working on a message series in our parish ("message series" are our weekend homilies organized around a single theme over the course of several weeks). And while we were grateful that God had protected Lydia, we realized we couldn't make sense of why God hadn't spared Christopher. Why did Tom and Pam have to suffer an unthinkable loss? It seemed completely random, and our faith isn't in a random God. The scriptures describe a God of order. And yet God's choices and decisions don't always make sense to us.

If you are a Christian, you may be very quick to defend God when terrible things happen to good people. You may feel the need to speak up for God in a secular culture that dismisses him easily. Or perhaps, as a believer, you gloss over this kind of criticism of God. It is easier not to think about such things. It is more convenient sometimes just to accept circumstances as you find them and events as they unfold. You want to move on with life "in faith": going to work, paying the bills, taking care of the kids, or whatever else fills your time. If so, this is a book for you because it will challenge you in terms of what you think you believe about God and how you respond when life doesn't make much sense.

If you are not a Christian or have stopped believing in Christianity, we are so glad you picked up this book—or accepted it from a friend—and actually cracked it open. Maybe you walked away from faith *precisely because* God didn't make sense to you; he seemed to be absent when *life* wasn't making much sense. You were told that you just had to have faith. And since you *didn't* have faith, you thought the only honest thing to do was to walk away. This is a book for you because it will speak exactly to those experiences.

Or maybe you are angry with God. It's true, you're mad at him. You were told or at least have heard that if you honored God, followed the commandments, and stayed out of trouble, you would be blessed with a good life. Nothing bad would ever happen to you or your loved ones. You kept the rules. You did everything the Church asked you to do; you did stay out of trouble, and then something bad happened anyway. God didn't hold up his end of the bargain, and you are angry with him for that. You feel cheated. This is a book for you too, because we know how you feel.

Perhaps you have never been introduced to God and what Christianity says about him. This is your first real chance to hear anything about God, and someone gave you this book as an introduction. This is definitely a book for you because it is a great place to start.

We do not pretend to have all the answers about God. No one does. If we did, then God would not be God. That said, we do hope to make a little more sense of him in the pages that follow. When questions and confusion, frustration and anger arise about where God is and what he's doing, we have nothing to fear. We don't have to run from those thoughts and emotions. We can lean into them. God is big enough to handle all that.

We're just two guys working in a parish in north Baltimore, a parish like many other parishes, with people like any other people. What follows are some of our stories and their stories and what we've learned about how God works in our lives and remains ever faithful to us. These stories speak to us, and we think they will speak to you too.

We invite you to read on as we try to make sense of what God is up to when life doesn't make sense and God seems to be missing.

IT MAKES SENSE THAT GOD DOESN'T MAKE SENSE

For as the heavens are higher than the earth
so are my ways higher than your ways,
my thoughts higher than your thoughts.

—Isaiah 55:9

A god small enough to be understood is not
big enough to be worshipped.

—Evelyn Underhill

Father Michael: Connor was probably the most delightful, positive student we ever had in our high school youth ministry program. While many students drop out after Confirmation, Connor not only remained a part of the program but he also became a student leader. And because of his gifts of personality, his peers flocked to our Sunday evening program. He was also a gifted artist and brought his skill to bear in some very interesting and original worship presentations here at church. Not incidentally, he was easily one of the best sacristans we've ever had, eventually rising to head sacristan, a position he held even after he began attending college locally.

In his sophomore year of college, we were experiencing some staff transitions, and I found myself shorthanded. Connor stepped up to the challenge and became a most helpful part-time assistant when not attending class. One Friday, about three weeks before Christmas, obviously a busy time of year, I had several commitments that took me rather far afield and late into the evening. Anticipating that this would be taxing, Connor volunteered to accompany me. After the last engagement, it was incredibly helpful that he could take the wheel for the drive home, during which, and much to my surprise, he really opened up about many things that were on his heart: his love for his family, his struggles with his faith despite his commitment to our parish, and his uncertainty about the future.

I would not soon forget the conversation, because just days later, Connor died, almost instantly, of an aneurysm.

Let's be honest. God often doesn't make sense. If you are not a religious person, this may be precisely why you don't go to church, believe the Bible, or even accept the reality of God. There are too many commandments that seem inconsistent; too much Church history that is indefensible; way too much going on in the world to reconcile with an all-loving God. Even if you are a follower of Jesus, it can be difficult to understand.

If you find yourself struggling at times with the question of God, *congratulations!* You are in good company. The heroes of the Bible frequently experienced situations in which they misunderstood or completely failed to understand God.

- Abraham couldn't comprehend why God gave him a son and then asked him to give up his son. *It didn't make any sense.*
- Moses, with his speech impediment and extreme shyness, was the least likely person ever to serve as God's chosen to lead Israel out of the slavery of Egypt. *It didn't make any sense.*
- David, a mere boy, was blindsided when God anointed him king. *It didn't make any sense.*
- The apostles, the closest friends and followers of Jesus, were constantly confused by his teaching and preaching. *It didn't make any sense.*

While God not making sense is nothing new, we offer you three important principles to keep in mind as you read this book.

FIRST PRINCIPLE: IT MAKES SENSE THAT GOD DOESN'T ALWAYS MAKE SENSE.

To put it bluntly, if those of us who believe in the God of the Bible have it right, then God is *smarter* and *older* than we are and *thinks* in ways far beyond our capacity.

God is smarter than we are.

The universe is unfathomably vast in its design but also incredibly intricate in its detail. The skill (for lack of a better word) needed to create the universe is unimaginable. As scientists study its exquisite, astonishing composition and complexity, the genius of creation is more and more revealed. And despite advances in these studies, scientists still do not even know what holds matter together.

Everything that *is* argues for an intelligent force behind creation. We call this force God. And while his wisdom, knowledge, and understanding are complete and comprehensive, ours is not.

> **Father Michael:** A few years ago we decided we needed to build a new church, as we had outgrown our existing sanctuary. I approached this project with excitement and enthusiasm, but little understanding of its complexity. The design phase was of great interest to me, and I followed it closely. But when it came to the engineering, electrical, mechanical, and all the other trades, I was lost. I eventually stopped going to the meetings, sending representatives instead, because I couldn't even follow the conversation. I knew what

I wanted the building to look like, but that's about all I knew.

If this sort of experience is so consistently and completely true in our interactions and conversations with one another, how could we expect it to be otherwise when it comes to our experience of God?

God is older than we are, knowing all times and cultures.

To say that God is older than us implies that God had a beginning, which he did not, of course, but language limits us. God is infinite. God stands outside of time, having created it. On the other hand, we are limited and defined (in part) by time. However long our life, we live according to a limited span, seeing love and loss and everyday experiences through this tiny window. God, on the other hand, sees all of human history at once.

> **Tom:** Michael and I were invited to Vienna to speak at a conference for Church leaders. We carved out a day before our speaking engagements to tour the city. As we visited the baroque Schönbrunn Palace, the magnificent Hofburg complex, and medieval St. Stephen's Cathedral, I found myself inspired by the history of it all. Pretty much everything I knew about Austria I learned from *The Sound of Music*, which of course depicts a moment in time just before the Second World War. I knew little of the Hapsburg dynasty, the Austro-Hungarian Empire, or the Holy Roman Empire that

> preceded it. I reflected that my sense of time is so
> often, in so many ways, limited.

Any view of the span of time can be instructive and even inspiring, but consider having a *complete* view, as one who stands outside of time. That is God's perspective, and God's alone.

God thinks differently than we do.

At one point in the Gospel of Matthew, Jesus rebukes his friend Peter, telling him, "You are thinking not as God does, but as human beings do" (Mt 16:23). Peter's problem is our problem. We think as human beings think. And you might wonder, *Well, how else am I supposed to think?* However, God doesn't actually want us to think only from a human perspective but to somehow try to see life from his perspective.

St. Paul called this the "renewal" of our minds (Rom 12:2). Paul's letter to the Romans reminds us that there is false thinking in every age. Each generation holds and forms errors in thinking. Therefore, we must beware of conforming our thinking to the common wisdom of our age and instead learn to think as God thinks.

So, how do we do that? Well, that leads us to a second principle we invite you to keep in mind.

SECOND PRINCIPLE: WE CAN GROW TO KNOW GOD'S THOUGHTS AND WAYS.

A group of blind men heard that a strange animal, called an elephant, had been brought to their village, but none of them was aware of its shape or form. Out of curiosity they said, "We must inspect and know it by touch, of which we are capable." So, they sought out the animal and, upon finding it, reached out to touch it. The first man's hand landed on the elephant's trunk and he said, "It is like a snake!" For another, whose hand reached its ear, the creature seemed like a kind of fan. A third, whose hand touched its leg, was sure this new creature was shaped like a tree trunk. The last of the group felt the tusk and imagined the elephant like a spear.

Many people might argue that this parable accurately describes the historical development of the great religions of the world. Different religions can understand different aspects of God, but no one knows the whole truth; we are all just guessing. So why even try to make sense of it?

You may feel the same way about God. You are not motivated to learn more because there are so many different viewpoints. If everyone is just guessing, then why study faith or religion at all unless you are simply doing it as an academic exercise? But Christianity responds to this parable by asking a question: *What if the elephant could talk?* What if the elephant began to describe each aspect of his body to help make sense of what the blind men were touching? The elephant could explain how his trunk and his tusks function, why he has thick legs and large ears, and so on.

Christianity argues that this is exactly what has happened when it comes to God. Christianity is not merely a religion dreamed up by human beings. Christianity is a *revelation*, the story of God revealing himself to friends and followers.

In the chapters that follow, we'll take a deeper look at some of this story, but here are the basics. God the Father revealed himself first and foremost to a particular people—the Jewish people—in a specific time and place. He revealed himself to a man, Abraham, who became a father and formed a family who grew into a tribe and eventually into a great nation. Then, over many centuries, God instructed this people about himself. Through the Law and the prophets, he taught them who he is, what he values, and how he wanted them to act. In the fullness of time, God revealed himself by sending his Son into the world. Jesus came to the earth to set us straight about God by being love in action. And then Jesus sent the Holy Spirit to continue to instruct us so that we can grow in our understanding and knowledge of God.

Even so, we have only a *partial* understanding about God. First and last, coming to know God is not simply a matter for the head but also for the heart. Christians believe that God is not just a concept but a divine, eternal communion of three persons. We grow to know God's thoughts and ways through a personal relationship with the Blessed Trinity—Father, Son, and Spirit.

THIRD PRINCIPLE: WE CAN'T CONFUSE *GOD* NOT MAKING SENSE WITH *LIFE* NOT MAKING SENSE.

Catholics pray the Our Father at every Mass. In that prayer Jesus taught us to say to God, *Thy will be done on earth as it is in heaven.* Why do we have to pray for God's will to be done? Because a lot of the time it isn't. God's will *isn't* always done on earth as it is always done in heaven. Heaven is perfect, and God's will reigns there.

Meanwhile, back here on planet Earth, many things that happen are *not* God's will. Of course you've heard well-meaning Christians explain sad and even tragic events with the trite phrase *It's God's will*. And you may have thought, *If that's God's will, then I want nothing to do with God*. We don't blame you. We agree with you. We wouldn't want to follow that God either.

But here's the truth we hold. God doesn't want injustice or poverty, violence or terrorism, disease or pandemics, hunger or homelessness. God doesn't *want* any of these things, but he *allows* them. Why?

Some theologians explain it this way: There is God's *preferred will* and his *permissive will*. God's preferred will is what he wants to happen, how he desires people to act. And yet God has given human beings freedom to act in a way that is contrary to what he wants. He gives us free will because only by using free will can we truly grow and actually learn to love.

> **Tom:** If you are a parent, you understand this well. You have a preferred will for your kids. You want them to act with kindness toward their siblings, take responsibility for their hygiene, do their schoolwork, and finish their chores. But often what I want is *not* what happens in my household, and I know that always demanding compliance is not a good long-term strategy for successful parenting.

If I want my kids to grow into mature adults, I can't
always *make* them do what is right.

The same is true for God. God is a loving Father who has
given us free will, and many things that don't make sense
in our world come from an *abuse* of free will. In its extreme
form we call this abuse evil, a force actually in opposition to
God. Christian thought has identified three major sources
of opposition to God's will: the world, the flesh, and the
devil. Let's work backward.

God is first of all opposed by the *devil*, a fallen angel
and the personification of evil. You may not believe in the
devil—the idea may seem like an old-fashioned fable, a religious myth designed to frighten. You are certainly not alone
in such views. Perhaps we can agree on this point: some of
the things that don't seem to make sense about God and our
world begin to make better sense when you posit that God's
will is opposed by a *personal being* of intelligence and free
will. We'll get back to this point later.

God's will is also opposed by the *flesh*. And by the flesh,
we mean you and me. Something in us resists God. Often
our actions don't rise to the level of intrinsic evil; they just
don't align with God's best for us. Other times, those bad
choices can and do bring negative consequences for ourselves, our families, and our community that are *actively
opposed* to God. They are evil. Either way, God honors us
enough to let us make those choices.

Finally, God's will is opposed by the *world*. What does
that mean? It simply means that parties and peoples, com-
mittees and countries that oppose God's will *individually*

come together *corporately* and form opposition. It is easy to recognize this when considering Nazi Germany, Stalinist Russia, or the Rwandan genocide. But the same can be true in any community or gathering given violent or extreme conditions. Then too, there are laws that are enacted, rules that are made, wars that are waged, that are flat-out wrong.

God's will is not done on this earth perfectly. His will is opposed. And yet, even so, when others intend evil, God can make all things work together for our good.

Those are the basics as we see it when it comes to God not making sense. With these principles in hand, let's move on to some of the specific ways we all struggle to make sense of God, especially when life seems not to make sense.

REFLECTION QUESTIONS

1. How might God be trying to reveal himself to you?

2. What questions do you have about God?

3. Have you ever had anyone answer your questions about God in a satisfactory way? If so, what has satisfied you?

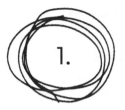

SERIOUSLY, *NO?*

And Jesus raised his eyes and said, "Father,
I thank you for hearing me. I know that you
always hear me."

—John 11:41–42

The greatest tragedy of life is not unanswered prayer, but unoffered prayer.

—F. B. Meyer

Tom: Growing up, I experienced mostly unanswered prayers. It is a little embarrassing to admit,
but in grade school and early middle school, my
prayers focused entirely on sports. I loved sports
more than anything else and would ask God to
bring success to me and my teams. In football
season, I begged that we would win regionals. In
basketball season, I prayed that we would sweep
the CYO championship. But my most earnest

prayers came in baseball season. Baseball was far and away my favorite sport, and I invested significant time in my team's success each spring. Yet we never won a single championship. Not once was that prayer answered.

Later, in high school, I had a huge crush on a girl in my class. I prayed fervently that God would warm her heart toward me. It became a pattern. I would renew this campaign with each new crush. (In case you're wondering, none of those prayers were answered either.)

I perhaps prayed most intensely as an adult during Super Bowl XXXIX when my hometown team, the Philadelphia Eagles, played the New England Patriots. I prayed the Eagles would win. Just for your information if you are not a football fan, they *didn't*. My prayers again went unanswered.

For whatever reason, the fact that my petitions were never answered did not fill me with cynicism or skepticism about prayer. I don't know why that was. Maybe I never really expected them to be answered. I looked at prayer as a way to express my hopes and dreams. Prayer was more or less wishful thinking, a lucky rabbit's foot, or a good-luck charm. It gave me confidence and a better chance of succeeding, but it was still just a shot in the dark. I was throwing my prayers up to heaven hoping they would succeed, seeing what would stick. I'd like to say I had a deep trust in God that

allowed me to accept no for an answer, but that
would be dishonest.

Only later in life did either of us come to see that prayer really can bring God's power into our life. Working at a parish, we have seen prayer make a difference and change outcomes over and over again. Prayer *does* work. Inviting God's power and intervention into our world *does* make a difference. Any Christian who has accomplished anything from Mother Teresa to Billy Graham to Rick Warren to Pope Francis would tell you that all the fruits of their work were accomplished in prayer. They have begged God for grace and favor, and they have seen him come through.

Prayer, though, isn't magic. Prayer is about entering into a relationship with a loving God. It doesn't assure us we will get what we want because God is not a genie in a bottle. God is the all-powerful, all-knowing sovereign ruler of the universe.

Musician Garth Brooks famously thanked God for unanswered prayers. Others say that God answers *all* prayers; it's just that sometimes the answer is no. God's responses to prayers have been compared to traffic lights. Sometimes God gives us a green light and says, "Go." He answers the prayer swiftly. Sometimes we get a yellow light, and God says, "Grow." We are asking God for the right thing, but we need to grow into the gift. Our prayer will be answered, but at the right time and in the right way. And sometimes God says, "No." He gives us a red light.

Tom: We can come to understand a no from God with the vantage point time provides. In retrospect, we can see that an earlier disappointment, like losing a baseball championship, helped build our character and make us more emotionally equipped to handle bigger disappointments later in life. In hindsight, being overlooked by a secret crush could leave the path open for the right person (as it did for me).

With time, there are some no answers that make sense to us, or make *more* sense, or at least don't seem like that big a deal in retrospect. But there are other issues we just can't understand; we'll never understand. God denies us an opportunity that we think would have fulfilled the deepest desires of our heart. We prayed fervently for an outcome or eventuality that would have been simply perfect. And it didn't happen, and we don't, we won't, ever understand why.

Of course, we have to be careful about this. Maybe we believe God has said no and it isn't *his* no at all. But sometimes God *does* tell us no. It becomes clear that it is God who has spoken. God tells us some things are just off limits. The question then becomes, *Why* does God tell us no? How each of us answers that question is very important in our personal relationship with God.

When it comes to God, we must make sure we have the right view of him, according to the biblical witness and the long tradition of the Church. Some people view God as a cosmic cop constantly watching us to see if we do something wrong. These people think of God as on the lookout for any time we bend the rules or break the laws. They think that God can't wait to catch us red-handed in wrongdoing and takes delight in punishing us when we make a mistake or step out of line. And, of course, according to this view, God *loves* to tell us no. God wants to make sure we stick to the narrow path and that means not having any fun at all. Many Catholics have grown up with this concept of God. Mass on Sunday was supposed to be boring and bad. The more it hurt, the better. It *counted* more if it was painful.

You may have left the Church because you were schooled in these views. You felt like the only answer you ever got from the Church and from God was no. All you heard was you aren't allowed to do *this*, don't do *that*, and no, you can't have that because God said so. If it was fun or brought joy to your heart, then that meant God was against it. And so the first chance you had, you got as far away from the Church and God as you could.

Or maybe you never went to Church at all because you saw it as a big obstacle to your freedom. The Christians you knew seemed to be defined by religious rule keeping and a harshly judgmental attitude toward those who didn't keep the same rules—although, at the same time, it was clear they kind of resented you for your freedom.

If this negative view is the lens through which you are interpreting things, then God's nos are never going to feel good or make any sense to you. They will seem spiteful, mean-spirited, and even vengeful on God's part.

Where some see a cosmic cop, others see a heavenly grandfather: distant, detached, and a little dotty. From this perspective, God's nos are an unexpected intervention that seems particularly unfair, an unnecessary intrusion into what you want to do.

Jesus didn't describe God in either of these ways. God is love. He is a loving Father who will do anything to get his kids home to heaven. So let's take a look at some of the reasons God, as a loving Father, will say no to us. And to start, we will look at a very familiar story.

THE FALL

This story comes to us from the book of Genesis, the very first book of the Bible. Many people view Genesis, especially the first few chapters, as a kind of fairy tale or children's story because we heard the story for the first time as children. We were introduced to it at the same time we were read bedtime stories about Sleeping Beauty or Thomas the Tank Engine. And, growing up, we left it behind in the nursery, perhaps to be revived with children of our own. Meanwhile, we learned that everything science tells us contradicts the creation stories of Genesis.

If you are an unchurched person or if you walked away from the Church, you might have left precisely because of books such as Genesis. You thought there was no way God could create the world in seven days, send a flood, and save the animals on an ark. And what happened to the dinosaurs? You walked away because you thought you couldn't be an intelligent person and believe in God or at least believe in the God of the Bible.

We believe in the truth of Genesis, even if we struggle to understand *how* it is true. While the narratives of Genesis are not intended to convey scientific facts, they are meant to tell us profound truths about who God is and who we are as the crown jewels of God's creation. Genesis was written with genius and subtlety. The form and content weave together truths about the origin of the universe, the nature of evil, and the struggles and challenges we face as human beings.

Genesis tells us that God created the world perfect. The phrase "God saw that it was good" (1:12) is used five times just to communicate this single truth. Genesis tells us that God created the world with perfect harmony. The first human beings were completely comfortable in their environment and with nature. They lived in a right relationship with God. They lived in a right relationship with one another.

When God had the world as he willed and wanted it, there was only one rule. People could not eat of the tree of the knowledge of good and evil—a tree whose fruit would impart knowledge of *everything*, including things God wanted to keep from his children. That was it. Everything else was allowed. Genesis conveys God's heart when it comes to rules. He likes to keep them simple and to a minimum.

God created the world good, and he created human beings *very* good. This raises two questions. If God created the world good, then why is it so very *not good?* Did God make a mistake? Genesis, chapter 3, tells us what happened to change all of that: "Now the snake was the most cunning of all the wild animals that the LORD God had made. He asked the woman, 'Did God really say, "You shall not eat from any of the trees in the garden"?'" (Gn 3:1). The snake is identified in the book of Revelation as the devil or Satan (Rv 12:9) and is the obvious villain in this story.

The serpent, the evil one, appropriately enough, twists God's words, suggesting the prohibition is much broader and more oppressive than it actually is. This, in turn, plants seeds of doubt in Eve's mind. The lie of evil is that a relationship with God brings slavery. The lie is that if we live apart from God, we will experience greater freedom when, in fact, the opposite is true. Our real freedom comes from living under God and the limits he sets for us.

The history of humanity is that we never do well when we set our own limits. We push our finances over the limit. We push our schedules over the limit. We push our relationships beyond their limits. So, we are often worn out, and played out, and eventually wasted, because we refuse to live within God's limits.

"The woman answered the snake: 'We may eat of the fruit of the trees in the garden; it is only about the fruit of the tree in the middle of the garden that God said, "You shall not eat or even touch it, or else you will die"'" (Gn 3:2–3). Eve is responding with a lie of her own, exaggerating God's prohibition in a different way ("or even touch it"). At this point she is already complicit in the serpent's scheme. He replies, "You certainly will not die! God knows well that when you eat of it your eyes will be opened and you will be like gods, who know good and evil" (Gn 3:4–5). This is what the evil one does. He works to steal our trust in God, to question God's intentions, to doubt God's love for us. The serpent tells Eve, *God is holding out on you. God is keeping good things from you. God doesn't want you to have these things because he really wants to control you.*

Evil whispers: *God has set these limits as an obstacle for you because he is against you. If you want to have the life you hope for, move beyond him and his silly, senseless rules. You can have God or a great life, but you can't have both.* This is the lie we buy over and over again. In every sin, we believe that the limits God has set are getting in the way of our fun, our success, our happiness.

Eve listened to the serpent. His way of thinking began to make sense, in a way God's law did not. Perhaps for the very first time, she looked at the fruit. Nothing seemed wrong with it: "The woman saw that the tree was good for food and pleasing to the eyes, and the tree was desirable for gaining wisdom" (Gn 3:6). This happens in life too. We see things. They are pleasing to the eye. They look good on the surface. They seem desirable for gaining something we want or achieving some goal we aspire to. Sometimes it is a person. They are attractive and engaging. They would make a great new friend. No matter that they are married, or that our loved ones have concerns about them. Or it may be a shiny new car, a bigger house, the latest fashion. It looks impressive. It makes us look impressive too. We want it. And we want to get it, despite the cost. No matter that our budget is already stretched beyond the breaking point and that we've racked up a pile of debt.

The fruit looks good. This will happen throughout life too. We see some good thing, and God says stay away from it. Don't touch it. Don't taste it. You really don't want to go near that. We think, *Why, God?* It looks really good. And it looks to be the opening or opportunity for more good things, too.

Adam and Eve knew what God said. But the fruit looked good, and there was a seed of doubt in their minds. So the next thing you know . . .

> She took some of its fruit and ate it; and she also gave some to her husband, who was with her, and he ate it. Then the eyes of both of them were opened, and they knew that they were naked; so they sewed fig leaves together and made loincloths for themselves. (Gn 3:6–7)

Suddenly their eyes were opened. And *as* their eyes were opened, everything changed for the worse. The perfect harmony that existed was gone in an instant. Their innocence was lost.

Eating the forbidden fruit and disobeying God's no caused a *threefold alienation*, damaging Adam and Eve and, by extension, all of us. The *first alienation* is from *ourselves*. As a result of sin, we are no longer comfortable in our own skin. Before the Fall, Adam and Eve were naked and felt no shame. Like little children, they had an innocence about their bodies. After eating the fruit and breaking God's only command, their eyes were opened, and their nakedness was uncomfortable. Their eyes were opened to their own vulnerability and human frailty.

Some biblical scholars suggest that before they sinned, Adam and Eve were clothed with God's glory. Once they ate the forbidden fruit, they lost the divine clothing. Before disobeying God, they had his divine protection around them; they had now broken with that protection. They were embarrassed by this sudden weakness. That's the first alienation, which leads to the *second alienation,* alienation from *God:* "When they heard the sound of the LORD God walking about in the garden at the breezy time of the day, the man and his wife hid themselves from the LORD God" (Gn 3:8).

When Adam and Eve hear God coming, they run and hide. Before the Fall, our first parents had an intimate relationship with God. He came to them in the garden in the cool part of the day. That's a great time of day in the summertime, especially at the beach, isn't it? The early evening has something special and especially relaxing about it. It is the time of day when our labor is complete and we can enjoy the fruits of our efforts. Before the Fall, Adam and Eve enjoyed this time with God, but now, instead of meeting with God, they run and hide from him. Their easygoing relationship with God is gone.

That's the nature of sin. When you have wronged someone or done something to hurt the relationship, you can't be comfortable around them, at least until you make amends. Lie or share gossip about someone, and suddenly their presence becomes menacing because they stand as a reminder of your sin. God's presence becomes a curse rather than a blessing to Adam and Eve.

This is why we so often avoid God and prayer. We know that in every sin, he is the one offended. The Fall alienated us from God. No longer is the relationship natural and easy. Genesis continues: "The LORD God then called to the man and asked him: Where are you?" (3:9). God knows exactly where Adam is physically. He is asking Adam to assess where he is *relationally*. He is asking Adam to evaluate his own situation and acknowledge his mistake, which Adam fails to do. Instead he evades: "He answered, 'I heard you in the garden; but I was afraid, because I was naked, so I hid.' Then God asked: Who told you that you were naked? Have you eaten from the tree of which I had forbidden you to eat?" (Gn 3:10–11). Since Adam doesn't admit the truth of eating the fruit, God calls it out. Whereas before, God and human beings could have an open, honest conversation with one another, now Adam is posturing. He is trying to hide what's really happening from God.

We do this as well. We pray prayers that don't really reveal what is going on in our hearts and in our lives. People who have a close relationship with God are incredibly honest with him. Read the psalms. David prays for success, and he prays for revenge. He shares his frustrations and his disappointments with God. He speaks honestly from his heart, and God loved his heart. God wants an honest relationship with us, but as a result of the Fall, we have a tendency to hide our true thoughts and feelings from him. We pretend that God cannot see us.

So after God calls out Adam for not being honest, does Adam acknowledge his mistake? No, instead he does something else: "The man replied, 'The woman whom you put here with me—she gave me fruit from the tree, so I ate it'" (Gn 3:12). Adam throws Eve under the bus and blames God as well. He basically says to God, *The woman* you *put here gave me the fruit. So, God, it's your fault for creating her and her fault for tempting me. I am not to blame.*

Before the Fall, Adam and Eve enjoyed the perfect relationship. They were naked with each other and felt no shame or distance. This wasn't just a physical nakedness but an emotional one as well; they could be honest and vulnerable. After the Fall, they become estranged from one another. This is the *third alienation*, the third result of sin and breaking the limitations God give us.

All the problems in the world come down to this three-fold alienation. We are uncomfortable with ourselves. We are not in a right relationship with God. And we are estranged from others. Fearing that our vulnerabilities will be exposed, we hide from God, we blame others, and we deceive ourselves.

Sin leads to fear and alienation. God did not create us this way, but it has become the "natural" state of affairs. We assume it is normal because that's the world we have inherited. But it is not what God intended. He had set a limit to protect us from that harm.

The problem is described another way later in the chapter: "Then the LORD God said: See! The man has become like one of us, knowing good and evil!" (Gn 3:22). Before eating the forbidden fruit, human beings knew only good. Now they know evil—not just intellectually but physically, spiritually, and relationally. On every level of their being, their lives have changed for the worse.

God tells us no sometimes, not because he is keeping something from us but because he doesn't want us to know evil. If you are a parent, you can relate to this. There are bad things out there you just don't want your kids to know about or, at least, not until they are old enough to process the reality of evil without being terribly harmed by it. You set rules and limits to protect your kids from evil. You are vigilant about how they use social media, what they watch on Netflix, and which video games they play. You want to know who they are texting and what friendships they are forming because there are plenty of bad influences around.

You say no to them. And you say it even though they don't always understand. It doesn't make sense to them. But you don't wait until they understand to impose the rule. You can't wait, because then it will be too late. They may complain. They may cry. They may cry foul. But it moves you not in the least. You know what you're doing. You know you are right. You know that you love them. And that is enough. God is a parent, just like you.

THE REBUKE

Sometimes God says no to protect us. But sometimes God says no to us for another reason. We discover a second reason in the Gospel of Mark.

All four gospels tell us the story of Jesus' life, but they tell it from different perspectives. Matthew and John were two of the twelve apostles, so they had a front-row seat to Jesus' life and mission. Luke was a physician who came to believe in Jesus because of the preaching of the apostle Paul. Eventually, he undertook research with eyewitnesses (including, according to some traditions, Jesus' mother, Mary) to write his gospel. Mark based his account on his relationship with the apostle Peter. Mark's gospel is the shortest of the four, so if you want to read one of the gospels from start to finish, it would be a good place to start. You could probably read the Gospel of Mark in less than an hour.

Mark tells us that at a certain point in his ministry, Jesus, with the twelve apostles, left the territory of Galilee to go to the region of the Gerasenes. To do so, they had to cross the Sea of Galilee. A huge squall arises, but they get through it (more on that story later). They arrive safely on the other side of the sea, but the apostles are met with a scary sight. Mark writes,

> They came to the other side of the sea, to the territory of the Gerasenes. When [Jesus] got out of the boat, at once a man from the tombs who had an unclean spirit met him. The man had been dwelling among the tombs, and no one could restrain him any longer, even with a chain. In fact, he had frequently been bound with shackles and chains, but the chains had been pulled apart by him and the shackles smashed, and no one was strong enough to subdue him. (Mk 5:1–4)

It's a spooky story, for sure. The territory of the Gerasenes is an eerie place. The land is rough and rocky, filled with caves that were used to bury the dead, so it would have been like landing the boat at a graveyard. Then, as soon as they step out of the boat, they are confronted by a deeply disturbed man. He is violent and uncontrollable; his body had marks of self-mutilation. He is an outcast from the community, raging among the dwellings of the dead.

Upon assessing the situation, the apostles might have been thinking, *Jesus, let's get back in the boat.* Some people don't follow Jesus because they think to do so would be boring. However, this conclusion is belied by reading the gospels. Jesus never bored anyone, and no disciple who followed him lacked for adventure. It is unfortunate that we church professionals have made the most interesting man who ever lived look boring.

The story continues:

> Catching sight of Jesus from a distance, he ran up and prostrated himself before him, crying out in a loud voice, "What have you to do with me, Jesus, Son of the Most High God? I adjure you by God, do not torment me!" (He had been saying to him, "Unclean spirit, come out of the man!") (Mk 5:6–8)

It quickly becomes clear that this man is suffering from possession by an evil spirit and that Jesus has traveled specifically to this place to heal him. The evil spirit is powerful and powerfully entrenched. And so healing the man was no simple task. Mark tells us that Jesus asked him, "'What is your name?' He replied, 'Legion is my name. There are many of us.' And he pleaded earnestly with him not to drive them away from that territory" (Mk 5:9–10). There is an unfolding power on display here. With power Jesus demands the spirit's name, compelling him to reply. Knowing his name brings still more power, sealing the spirit's fate. Finally, the spirit's plea is a negotiation of his loss.

Now you might be skeptical of this idea, especially if you don't believe in evil spirits. But have you ever noticed that naming your negative emotions can weaken their power over you? Just saying "I am angry" can help diminish your anger. And when you are most angry, you may yell, "I'm not angry!" It's as if denying it makes you even angrier.

The same can be true of fear. You feel afraid but are reluctant to say you are afraid. Yet once you speak it out, it begins to lose its power. A classic example of this comes in *Rocky III*. The whole arc of the movie changes when Rocky confesses to Adrian, "All right, I'm afraid. For the first time in my life, I'm afraid."

Anger and fear are not just emotions. There is a spirit behind them. You don't have to believe in spirits to prove it to yourself. The next time you are angry or afraid, name it and see if that doesn't lessen its power.

This spirit's name is Legion. This was a military term: a legion equaled about six thousand men. So this guy doesn't just have one problem. He has a mighty host of problems.

> Now a large herd of swine was feeding there on the hillside. And they pleaded with him, "Send us into the swine. Let us enter them." And he let them, and the unclean spirits came out and entered the swine. The herd of about two thousand rushed down a steep bank into the sea, where they were drowned. (Mk 5:11–13)

Please don't get caught up in animal-rights considerations. Jesus didn't condemn the swine; the evil spirits did. Jesus allows the demons to leave the man, upon which they choose to enter the swine, who immediately run off a cliff, fall into the sea, and drown. The sea in scripture sometimes stands for a place of evil, so that's why the swine, considered by Jews to be unclean, run there.

But notice how easily the evil spirits are defeated. Once Jesus knows their name, all he has to do is command them to leave, and they must obey. This story shows Jesus' power to defeat evil *quickly*. Sometimes we battle with evil and the fight becomes protracted. We undertake the fight armed only with our own power. Inviting Jesus and his power into the battle would lead to a much quicker victory.

> The swineherds ran away and reported the incident in the town and throughout the countryside. And people came out to see what had happened. As they approached Jesus, they caught sight of the man who had been possessed by Legion, sitting there clothed and in his right mind. And they were seized with fear. (Mk 5:14–15)

So the swineherds run back into the town to tell everyone what happened, and a crowd of people come to see for themselves. The man who had been possessed to the point of raving insanity now looks completely normal. The people are terrified. You would be too. This kind of power on display would be frightening. Jesus' actions have created quite a stir.

Mark tells us the man is *sitting*, further illustrating the peace now present in a previously violent person. The town could do nothing with this man but chain him up, and even their chains could not constrain him. One moment the man is mad to the point of literally pulling apart shackles and hurting himself, and in the next moment he is completely calm. He is at peace. Jesus comes to restore the man to his right mind and his rightful place in the community. We cannot solve our human problems with human solutions. We need God's divine power.

From here the story takes an interesting twist: "Those who witnessed the incident explained to them what had happened to the possessed man and to the swine. Then they began to beg him to leave their district" (Mk 5:16–17). Jesus had just healed this man. He had done something that no one thought possible. A man who was completely out of control, a danger to himself and a menace to the community, had been healed and put back into his right mind. Rather than wanting to know more about this stranger who had such incredible power, the Gerasenes beg Jesus to go. Why? They are afraid. His power is too much for them. We often see this reaction to Jesus in Mark's gospel. People are filled with awe in the presence of Jesus' power.

The people beg Jesus to leave, and he complies. He doesn't force himself on them. He doesn't protest, and he doesn't get offended. He simply gets back in the boat. And as he gets back in the boat, the man Jesus healed asks him to go along. You would think that if someone wanted to go with Jesus, he would say yes; that if someone was eager to be with Jesus and follow him around, of course he would agree. But, as you might have guessed from the title of this chapter, that's *not* how Jesus answers: "He would not permit him but told him instead, 'Go home to your family and announce to them all that the Lord in his pity has done for you'" (Mk 5:19). Jesus loves the possessed man enough to restore him to health. He also loves him enough to give him a mission to undertake now that he is healed. He loves the man, but he also loves all the other people in the community. Jesus wants them to know the Good News too. So, he sends the man back into the community as his ambassador, his emissary.

The people of Gerasa were not ready to interact directly with Jesus. They were frightened by him. So Jesus sends this man, whose life has changed, to speak for him. He sends him home to share his encounter with Jesus because, though people can challenge your beliefs and reject your creed, no one can deny you your story.

Jesus tells the man no because by staying behind, he can have a positive impact on his community, by simply telling his story. And that's what happened: "Then the man went off and began to proclaim in the Decapolis what Jesus had done for him; and all were amazed" (Mk 5:20). The man tells his story, and the people move from *fear* to *faith*. Later, Mark's gospel tells us that when Jesus returned to that same land, a crowd of people who had become believers came out to hear him speak and to be healed by him. One guy's testimony of what Jesus did for him changed many in the community.

So, maybe you have been trying to leave someplace. You have been looking for a new place to work. You don't like the people in your office, or you feel like you are stuck in a dead-end job. And you keep feeling God's no in the rejection letters or lack of callbacks. But there are people in your office who could benefit from their relationship with you. They could come to know Jesus because of your story.

Maybe you feel stuck in your current house. You would rather live in a different neighborhood, but you can't sell your house, or you just don't have enough money to move. You feel like it is a big no from God. But in your neighborhood there may be someone who needs to hear your story and about your relationship with Jesus or about your struggles to believe. Maybe God wants you to influence them, and that's why you can't move.

Maybe you are trapped in the wrong school; at least it feels that way some days. You wish you were somewhere else. You wish you were anywhere else. It seems so unfair, and it seems as though God doesn't care. But God has a plan and a purpose for you there when it comes to influencing other students.

Sometimes God says no to protect us. Sometimes God says no to redirect us. And then, every once in a while, he says no to bless us.

Tom: Super Bowl XXXIX wasn't the only time that my prayers were focused on the Philadelphia Eagles. As I mentioned earlier, I grew up in Philadelphia and was raised to be a huge Eagles fan. My passion for the Eagles came from watching games with my dad. On Sunday afternoons in the fall, this was a key way we connected. He loved watching games from the comfort of his couch with me. When I went away to college, my dad wrote to me lamenting that without me around, he had to watch the Eagles all by himself.

While my dad liked watching games on his couch, I like being at the games. So when the Eagles won the NFC championship in 2018, I made it my mission to get a ticket to the Super Bowl. I found a friend in the parish, TJ, who said he would go too. I used points to reserve a flight out to Minnesota where the game would take place. All I needed was a ticket to the game. I had a few contacts that I thought might make it possible for me to secure a ticket at a somewhat reasonable cost. I prayed that God would open up an avenue to find a ticket and believed he would. While you might find it surprising that I would ask God for a ticket to a game, I don't think there is any limit to the prayers he will grant. I view God as a loving Father who loves to give good things to his kids the same way I do—so why not ask for a ticket?

I kept praying, but finally I got to the Saturday before the game and no ticket, even though I had some near misses. On Saturday morning, TJ called me up to see what I wanted to do. Maybe we should fly out there and something would come through. He said it was my call. I felt in my spirit that just wasn't the right thing to do.

Now I had to figure out where to watch the game. I was disappointed and needed a plan B. I thought the next best thing would be to make the ninety-minute drive from Baltimore to Philly to watch the game with my dad. So that's what I did.

If you know anything about that Super Bowl, you know it was an incredible back-and-forth game. There were dramatic plays from the famous "Philly Special" to Brandon Graham's strip sack of Tom Brady. It culminated with an incomplete Hail Mary pass that fell to the ground as time ran out. The Eagles emerged Super Bowl champions for the first time in their history. My dad and I celebrated and rejoiced together.

At the same time, it was a little bittersweet. I wanted to be at the game. I could have been there in person, and I wasn't. It had me a little bit upset with God. I know it was a small thing, but God is the king of the universe, and if he wanted, he could have gotten me a ticket.

Six months later, my dad suffered a heart attack, and within days he died. As difficult as it was, he was surrounded by his loved ones. It was a peaceful, prayerful passing. He lived a great life and has a living legacy in nineteen grandchildren. I was able to give his eulogy after the funeral Mass. Of course, in the months after his death, I continued to think about his life and the last few times we had together. Then one day, I finally realized that I had watched hundreds of Eagles games with my dad but the very last one was the Eagles' Super Bowl victory.

It's one of my favorite, cherished memories. If God had given me a ticket, I would not have watched that last game with my dad. Sometimes God says no because he has something better in store for us.

REFLECTION QUESTIONS

1. What evidence do you have from your life that shows that God answers prayers?

2. Name an evil you don't want your children to know. How does this help us understand some of God's nos?

3. When has a no from God redirected you? When has a no from God turned out to be a blessing?

SERIOUSLY, YOU LET ME DOWN!

Do not forsake me, O LORD;
my God, be not far from me!

—Psalm 38:22

Scarlett: Rhett, where should I go? What
should I do?
Rhett: Frankly, my dear. I don't give a
damn.

—*Gone with the Wind*

Tom: I have a big family of eight kids who range
in age from nineteen to one. Harmony and good
order are tenuous in the very best of times. But
on this particular day, my wife, Mia, was away, and
the situation was already complete chaos before

25

I had even left for work. The "plan" was for my older kids to babysit the little ones while I was at church. I somehow made it out of the house leaving behind a modicum of civility, hoping it might last. I arrived at the office for our Sunday morning check-in late (to the annoyance of others) and distracted. I remained distracted throughout the morning, texting questions and instructions to my three teenage boys and hearing nothing in response.

Angry and annoyed, I slipped out between Masses and raced home to find out what was going on. To my partial relief, the kids had not burned down the house. But neither were they using their time well. Everyone was just hanging out on their devices, playing video games. It was a beautiful summer day, and I wanted the older ones to take the younger ones to the pool and get them lunch. I knew they would spend the rest of the day in front of screens if I didn't insist. A huge fight ensued without clear battle lines, everyone getting involved. Eventually I prevailed (sort of) and took off, hoping I was not too late for an important meeting at church.

While driving back on the Baltimore beltway, all of a sudden I noticed a warning light blinking on the dashboard of my minivan. (Yes, a minivan. When you have eight kids, people are always asking you what you drive. We have two minivans.) It was a light announcing low tire pressure. With only that much warning, it became completely clear that I had a flat tire.

I realized I had to take the next exit because otherwise I was going to have to change a tire on an extremely busy interstate highway with cars whizzing by me at seventy-five miles an hour. So I got off as soon as I could, pulled into the empty lot of a nearby church, and called Michael to come and pick me up.

Father Michael: When I arrived at the lot, Tom's van was jacked up at a precarious angle and he was underneath, struggling to remove the flat tire. The van rocked back and forth, and the situation looked dangerous. I urged him to get out from underneath the vehicle, and when he emerged, he was soaking wet and filthy. Long story short, we got into a fight about his mad dash home. We missed an important meeting, and we missed out on soliciting a significant contribution from a donor who could have underwritten a major initiative we had long been planning.

St. Teresa of Avila is alleged to have complained to God after one particularly difficult and disappointing day, "If this is how you treat your friends, it's no wonder you have so few of them."

Storms are inevitable. Trials and tribulations, hardships, hassles, headaches, heartaches are a normal part of life—the rule, not the exception. You're likely either in a storm right now, headed into one, or headed out of one. And yet they constantly catch us off guard. When we hit an unexpected storm or an unexpected succession of storms, it can often feel like God has betrayed us. We're living our life, doing our job, saying our prayers, and going to church. We're keeping faith; we're being faithful. We're holding up our end of the arrangement, and he's letting us down. He has allowed a problem into our life, and it always seems to come at the worst time. It can feel like betrayal.

Scripture describes two famous storms that precisely illustrate the point.

JONAH'S STORM

The first example comes from an Old Testament story in the book of Jonah. You've probably heard the story of Jonah and the whale. If ever there was an improbable fish story, this is it. But we need not approach it as a historical account.

The word *Bible* means "library." The Bible is a compilation of different books. In those books we discover different forms of literature. Think of the Bible like a bookcase in your home. On your shelves you might have works of fiction, nonfiction, poetry, and biography. The Bible's like that. The gospels are eyewitness testimonies. This is why they are filled with small, seemingly insignificant details. They are the written accounts of people's memories.

Other parts of the Bible, such as the story of Jonah, can be approached as allegories or parables. You don't have to accept the details of the story of Jonah to discover truth, real truth, that holds permanent value. To call a book an allegorical tale does not diminish its power or importance.

For example, no one really believes Ebenezer Scrooge existed as a person. *A Christmas Carol* is a fictional story, an allegory about the importance of generosity and the trap of greed and bitterness. And yet if you say to someone, "Don't be a Scrooge," most of us know exactly what that means. No one stops to question whether Scrooge really existed. That Scrooge was an invention of Charles Dickens is beside the point; you understand the meaning of the term.

Christians believe the story of Jonah was inspired by the Holy Spirit to teach spiritual truths. Even if you are not a Christian, or don't believe the Holy Spirit inspired the story, you can benefit from it just as you benefit from your favorite novels or movies. Stories are sticky. We remember them. When we hear a story, it sparks our imagination to think about how we would act in a given situation. This is why Jesus used parables and stories in his teaching all the time. Perhaps there was not literally a "good Samaritan" as Jesus described (Lk 10:29–37), and yet the story presents a challenge to act like the good Samaritan. Stories can convey powerful and memorable messages, as we see in the book of Jonah. So let's dive into it.

The story begins with God telling Jonah to go to the city of Nineveh: "The word of the LORD came to Jonah, son of Amittai: Set out for the great city of Nineveh, and preach against it; for their wickedness has come before me" (Jon 1:1–2). Nineveh was located on the east side of the Tigris River and established as the capital of the Assyrian Empire

by Sennacherib seven hundred years before Christ. The people of Nineveh were enemies of Israel and known for their
brutality. For example, one of their kings' preferred form
of torture was tearing off the lips and hands of his defeated
enemies. Another perfected the "skill" of flaying a person
(peeling off the skin) while keeping them alive for extended
periods of time. Basically, the Assyrians were a cruel, powerful people feared and despised by the Israelites.

God instructs Jonah to go to precisely these people and
tell them that the Lord has seen their wickedness. Jonah is
to let them know that while they think God is indifferent to
their brutality, he sees it and wants it to stop.

Let's pause on this for a moment. Often, we become
angry with God because he seems to ignore evil actions or
not notice bad behavior. The book of Jonah, like other books
of the Bible, teaches us that God *does* notice. And over and
over again, he sends his servants and prophets like Jonah
to warn the wicked to change their ways. The people may
not listen to the prophets, but God does send them. Jonah's
story provides a bit of a twist to that theme: "He went down
to Joppa, found a ship going to Tarshish, paid the fare, and
went down in it to go with them to Tarshish, away from the
LORD" (Jon 1:3). Nineveh was to the east, and Jonah went
west. He doesn't just ignore the Lord or refuse to obey him.
Jonah deliberately runs away from the Lord's will and way.
Why did he do that? At this point in the story we don't know.

> The LORD, however, hurled a great wind upon the sea,
> and the storm was so great that the ship was about to
> break up. Then the sailors were afraid and each one cried

to his god. To lighten the ship for themselves, they threw its cargo into the sea. Meanwhile, Jonah had gone down into the hold of the ship, and lay there fast asleep. (Jon 1:4–5)

The Lord sends a storm into Jonah's path. The storm is so great that the sailors fear the ship will be totally destroyed and that they will be lost. They cry out to their gods, suggesting that they do not know about the God of Israel. In a desperate attempt to save themselves, they dispose of the cargo weighing them down. Presumably, the cargo was valuable, so this sacrifice indicates that they are seriously scared. They are doing everything they possibly can to keep the boat from sinking. And what is Jonah doing? He is asleep.

The captain wakes Jonah up and tells him to pray: "What are you doing asleep? Get up, call on your god! Perhaps this god will be mindful of us so that we will not perish" (Jon 1:6). The time for captaining the ship is over. All the captain can do now is pray and beg for God's mercy.

The crew decides that God must be mad at someone on board and that they are all being punished: "They said to one another, 'Come, let us cast lots to discover on whose account this evil has come to us.' So they cast lots, and the lot fell on Jonah" (Jon 1:7). Jonah then confesses that he is running from God. He knows that God has sent this storm to compel him to change direction. The captain asks Jonah what to do. "Jonah responded, 'Pick me up and hurl me into the sea and then the sea will calm down for you. For I know that this great storm has come upon you because of me.' Still the men rowed hard to return to dry land, but they could not, for the sea grew more and more stormy" (Jon 1:12–13).

Jonah tells the men it's his fault. They are in trouble because of what he has done wrong, because he turned from God. This is the nature of sin. There is no such thing as "private sin." The argument that "it isn't hurting anyone" is flawed. Usually you don't have to dig too far to see that sin causes harm to others. Our acts of selfishness and turning from God have repercussions. That's just the uncomfortable fact.

Jonah acknowledges his fault and embraces his deserved punishment. However, the captain and his crew don't want to send him to a certain death, so they keep struggling to survive. While Jonah the supposed God-follower has acted selfishly and put other people in danger, those who do not know God model godly behavior. One interesting theme in the book of Jonah is that Gentiles, the "pagans," act with nobility and righteousness—a new idea at the time that anticipates Christ's message of God's universal love and mercy.

After these failed efforts, the captain and his men decide to listen to Jonah:

> Then they cried to the LORD: "Please, O LORD, do not let us perish for taking this man's life; do not charge us with shedding innocent blood, for you, LORD, have accomplished what you desired." Then they picked up Jonah and hurled him into the sea, and the sea stopped raging. (Jon 1:14–15)

The captain and his crew ask for mercy, having made a difficult decision. They sacrifice one for the good of all. And just like that, the storm stops raging, the sea ceases its surging. These men, who do not know God, make a sacrifice to him and pledge their lives to him, because they have gone through this storm.

And what happens to Jonah? "The LORD sent a great fish to swallow Jonah, and he remained in the belly of the fish three days and three nights" (Jon 2:1). It's like putting a kid in timeout.

A question to ask ourselves when in a storm is what God is trying to *teach* us. It may be wisdom that this particular experience offers. But wisdom does not come only from experience. You know plenty of people who have had a great many experiences but have not grown wise. Wisdom comes from *evaluated* experience. Wisdom and insight are the fruits of stepping back and *reflecting* on our experiences as Jonah reflects on his. And the fruit of his contemplation? The biblical story tells us that the Lord heard and answered Jonah, "Out of my I distress I called to the LORD and he answered me; From the womb of Sheol I cried for help, and you heard my voice" (Jon 2:3).

Running away from God is never a strategy for long-term success. God sometimes interrupts our plans or allows them to fall and fail on their own because he wants to save us from ourselves. Through his time of contemplation, Jonah recognizes that God has actually shown mercy toward him. He realizes that God allowed, in fact *sent*, the storm to redirect him. He comes to understand that God had raised the storm to save him from his disobedience. Sometimes God sends the storm not to *pay* you back but to *bring* you back. The storm was actually an expression of God's love.

But our friend Jonah has still more to learn:

> Then the LORD commanded the fish to vomit Jonah upon dry land.
>
> The word of the LORD came to Jonah a second time: Set out for the great city of Nineveh, and announce to it the message that I will tell you. (Jon 2:11–3:2)

So, second verse, same as the first. God tells Jonah, let's try this again. You have another chance. Set out for the city of Nineveh and give them my message. This time Jonah obeys. "Jonah set out for Nineveh, in accord with the LORD. Now Nineveh was an awesomely great city; it took three days to walk through it. Jonah began his journey through the city . . . announcing, 'Forty days more and Nineveh shall be overthrown'" (Jon 3:3–4).

Nineveh, modern-day Mosul in northern Iraq, was a big city in the ancient world, so it took three days for Jonah to walk through it (the same amount of time he spent in the belly of the fish). Interestingly, Jonah doesn't say *why* the city will be overthrown or destroyed, just *when*. The implication is that the Ninevites themselves knew. They recognized their sins and understood their disobedience. The violence and hedonism of their culture are often considered unparalleled in human history. They knew in their consciences that they were living as they should not. They didn't even need to be told. Often, that's the case with us. We know what we have done wrong.

> The people of Nineveh believed God; they proclaimed a fast and all of them, great and small, put on sackcloth.
>
> When the news reached the king of Nineveh, he rose from his throne, laid aside his robe, covered himself with sackcloth, and sat in ashes. Then he had this proclaimed throughout Nineveh: "By decree of the king and of his nobles, no man or beast, no cattle or sheep, shall taste anything; they shall not eat, nor shall they drink water. Man and beast alike must be covered with sackcloth and call loudly to God; they all must turn from their evil way and from the violence of their hands." (Jon 3:5–8)

The people of Nineveh believed God. Even the king believed God! It was unbelievable! This was truly remarkable since the Assyrian kings were brutal despots; they had to be in order to hold on to power. That this king would subject himself and his realm to such a humble act of penance was, well, unbelievable. Humbly he prays, "Who knows? God may again repent and turn from his blazing wrath, so that we will not perish" (Jon 3:9).

This sentiment echoes throughout scripture when people act humbly and with faith before the Lord. Who knows what God will do with my fasting? Who knows what God will do with my act of service? Who knows what God will do with my prayer? Who knows what God will do as a result of my giving? The king says, "I don't know how God will respond. God doesn't owe us anything, but perhaps he will change his mind and not give us the punishment we deserve. Perhaps God will respond in a way that will bring good things into our lives."

This humility has an impact on God throughout the Bible. It is impressive in this story and others how God allows humans to influence him, affect him, move him, and even push him to "change" his mind. "When God saw by their actions how they turned from their evil way, he repented of the evil he had threatened to do to them; he did not carry it out" (Jon 3:10).

Of course, we really have to ask ourselves, was God changed or were the Ninevites changed through their exercise of humility? When we choose to use it, humility can change the circumstances of most any situation. If we approach someone confidently but without a sense of entitlement, they are more likely to respond to our requests.

So, Jonah ran away from God. God had mercy on him. Jonah obeyed God, and told the people of Nineveh to repent. The people repented and God accepted their repentance. All is good, right? Not quite.

You see, Jonah is now angry . . . at God. In Jonah 4:1 we learn, "This greatly displeased Jonah and he became angry." Sometimes we get angry at God because our plans don't work out. We run in the opposite direction and then blame God for our situation. Proverbs 19:3 tells us, "Their own folly leads people astray; in their hearts they rage against the LORD." When we get mad at God and our hearts rage against him, we would be wise to pause and reflect on this verse. Am I angry at God for what I have done? Am I in trouble because I knowingly did something wrong?

Father Michael: The most striking example of that here at the parish came in staffing. We did not have a large staff when I came here as pastor but some of those we had were deeply dysfunctional. Consequently, I was quietly relieved when most of them left in my first two years (for a variety of reasons, not a few in protest of me and new policies and procedures I was introducing). Anyway, this gave me the perfect opportunity to build my own team. Unfortunately, I proceeded to do so without pausing to consider what I had learned through those difficulties and departures. Neither did I turn to prayer or seek the wisdom and guidance of more experienced pastors. I simply staffed up quickly and somewhat thoughtlessly and, in the process, actually repeated the problems I'd inherited. There was the music director who insisted on playing music nobody liked, the disinterested and disengaged DRE, and the list went on.

Of course, at first, I worked hard to try and overlook my mistakes or just ignore them. But eventually I had to acknowledge I had a problem of my own making. But far from taking responsibility, even at that point, I turned to recrimination . . . I turned to the Lord with recriminations. At one point I actually prayed "Why don't you give me the people I need? It's all your fault!"

So often we have a goal in mind and a plan to proceed in a certain manner and then something gets in our way. We get angry. We get annoyed. Sometimes we grow angry and annoyed at rules or laws, at bureaucrats or bureaucracies that hold us up or shut us down. And sometimes we get angry and annoyed at *God* because he gets in our way. We get angry at anyone who gets in our way. But if we are headed in the wrong direction, pushback by God—often through the gift of loved ones—is truly an act of mercy and love.

The next verse (Jon 4:2) of the story tells us why Jonah ran from God in the first place. It reveals something Jonah was thinking all along but had remained hidden until this point of the narrative. Jonah prayed, "O LORD, is this not what I said while I was still in my own country? This is why I fled first toward Tarshish. I knew that you are a gracious and merciful God, slow to anger, abounding in kindness, repenting of punishment."

Jonah didn't want to go to Nineveh because he knew of God's love and mercy and he didn't want his enemies to experience it. As an aside, this description of God appears in several books of the Old Testament: Exodus, Psalms, Nehemiah, and Joel, as well as here in the book of Jonah. People often think of the "God of the Old Testament" as an angry God, but the scriptures most often present God as "gracious, merciful, slow to anger and abounding in kindness."

Jonah was a prophet, and he knew this about God. He recognized God's mercy and didn't want it extended to the Ninevites. Has that ever happened to you in a relationship? You know how someone acts, how they respond in certain situations. You try to manipulate the situation to get them to act differently. And when they don't, when they respond exactly as you knew they would, you get angry with them.

I knew it—I knew you were going to give them the money.

I knew it—I knew you were going to change your mind.

I knew it—I knew you were going to let them get away with it, *again*.

You might be thinking, *But didn't God show mercy to Jonah when he was disobedient? Isn't Jonah being a bit inconsistent, even hypocritical?* Ah, yes. And look at where it leads him: "So now, LORD, please take my life from me; for it is better for me to die than to live" (Jon 4:3). Biblical scholars have a term for Jonah: drama queen. God responds with a very piercing question: "Are you right to be angry?" (Jon 4:4). Another translation says, "Do you do well to be angry?" In other words, How's that working for you? How is your anger at my kindness and mercy adding value to your life? Should the same kindness and mercy I extended to you be withheld from others?

Jonah doesn't answer the question. Instead, he runs away *again*. Out of the city and at a distance, he waits to see what will happen. Maybe God will still destroy Nineveh. Instead, God has one more lesson for him.

> Then the LORD God provided a gourd plant. And when it grew up over Jonah's head, giving shade that relieved him of any discomfort, Jonah was greatly delighted with the plant. But the next morning at dawn God provided a worm that attacked the plant, so that it withered. (Jon 4:6–7)

God shows mercy *again* to Jonah by letting a plant grow quickly and provide him shade. But then the plant dies just as quickly. When the sun rises the next morning, the heat overwhelms Jonah, but in his stubbornness he refuses to move.

"But God said to Jonah, 'Do you have a right to be angry over the gourd plant?' Jonah answered, 'I have a right to be angry—angry enough to die'" (Jon 4:9). Jonah stands on his rights. He has a right to be angry because the people of Nineveh are terrible people. They *should* be destroyed by God, and God isn't destroying them. Jonah's self-absorption and sense of self-righteousness stand in stark contrast to God's mercy.

> Then the LORD said, "You are concerned over the gourd plant which cost you no effort. . . . And should I not be concerned over the great city of Nineveh, in which there are more than a hundred and twenty thousand persons who cannot know their right hand from their left?" (Jon 4:10–11)

In other words, God says to Jonah, "You care so much about this plant because it gave you comfort. How much more important are people, who are all my children? They were lost, and I sent you to help them find their way because *my* people are so much more important than your comfort."

The story ends abruptly with a challenging question: "Should I not be concerned?" The question is posed not to irreligious people, not to people who don't have a relationship with God, but to Jonah and everyone else who does.

Storms disrupt our comfort, our patterns, our routine. Storms can overturn our expectations; they can challenge us out of our preconceptions. And we can get mad at God for that. But storms also have the potential to remind us of what is important to God. God values love and mercy and kindness and patience. Most of all, God values people—all people. People are most important to him.

You know that. We know that. But sometimes we need to go through storms and face problems to be *reminded* about that truth of God's character. Sometimes God sends a storm to remind you of something you already know.

And sometimes he sends you into a storm to take your understanding of him to a whole new level. We see that in the next story.

THE APOSTLES' STORM

"On that day, as evening drew on, [Jesus] said to them, 'Let us cross to the other side'" (Mk 4:35). The evening that Mark describes in the fourth chapter of his gospel was the end of a long day of preaching and teaching. Jesus had been speaking from a boat just off the shore of the Sea of Galilee. He had attracted a huge crowd and spoke to them at considerable length. For some reason—perhaps in order to disperse the crowd in an efficient manner—when he was finished teaching he proposed to his apostles that they cross to the other side of the sea.

An unexpected request certainly, but not exactly a dramatic one—so far. As we'll read, they sail straight into a crisis. Any story worth telling offers some difficulty or challenge at the outset. Good stories include conflict to enter and obstacles to overcome. If our lives are to be stories worth telling, we are going to face storms.

So the apostles hit a storm. Sometimes, we get in trouble and it is *our* fault. Like Jonah, we make a bad decision, a poor choice, a big mistake. We decide to borrow more than we should, stay out too late, drink one too many. Problems like these are all of our making and we have nobody to blame but ourselves. Like Jonah, we are operating outside of God's will. But some storms come our way because we are doing God's will. We are trying to be both good parents and good employees. We are trying to manage both our personal health and our responsibility to others. We are trying to be generous with our resources but good stewards of our money at the same time.

The apostles hit a storm. But here is the thing—it wasn't *their* idea. It was Jesus' idea. He proposed crossing at night, which was risky in itself. He led them into a storm. That's what doesn't make sense to us. We can understand getting into trouble when we do something wrong or are outside God's will. It is more difficult to accept challenges and storms *inside* God's will that God leads us into.

"Leaving the crowd, they took him with them in the boat just as he was. And other boats were with him" (Mk 4:36). This little detail of the other boats adds nothing to the story. So why is it included? Because it really happened. The event we are looking at, as fantastic as it sounds, had eyewitnesses to testify to its veracity. Little details like that get thrown into a story because people who went through the event shared that detail when they shared their story.

Suddenly, a huge storm arises: "A violent squall came up and waves were breaking over the boat, so that it was already filling up" (Mk 4:37). Storms are pretty common in that region. The Sea of Galilee sits seven hundred feet below sea level, and just thirty miles to the north is Mount Hermon, which stands ninety-two hundred feet high. The cold air from the mountains continually clashes with warm air coming up from the sea, resulting in impressive and frightening thunderstorms.

The boat begins filling up with water so that it looks like it is going to sink. Neither of us are big boat people, nor have we ever experienced a storm at sea. Maybe some of you can relate to the experience of being in such a storm, but either way we can all appreciate the idea of being overwhelmed by our circumstances when we feel that life is out of control, that drowning is a real possibility.

Maybe that's your experience right now. You're drowning just trying to meet your financial obligations: student loans, credit card debt, car payments. You're drowning in your family responsibilities, with aging parents or little kids or maybe both. You're drowning in stress and tension, anxiety, depression. Maybe the problems aren't in just one area of your life; sometimes it seems like the whole of your life consists of balancing work and marriage, keeping up with home repairs and housework, or meeting the expectations of friends, family, and extended family. You feel like your boat is filling up, and you don't know what to do. That's where the apostles are. They don't really know what to do.

The story continues: "Jesus was in the stern, asleep on a cushion. They woke him and said to him, 'Teacher, do you not care that we are perishing?'" (Mk 4:38). Through the storm, Jesus is asleep, just like Jonah. The only reference anywhere in the four gospels to Jesus sleeping is in the midst of this storm. He is asleep on a cushion. Why is that insignificant detail included? Because he was asleep on a cushion. Again, just the sort of detail an eyewitness would mention.

The apostles wake up Jesus urgently. It's likely that they don't expect Jesus to do anything about the problem; what could he possibly do, anyway? They wake him up because they want him to share their distress. They wake him for the same reason you tell people about your problems. We share our problems sometimes not because we think someone can solve them but because it just feels better.

> **Tom:** After that flat tire wrecked the rest of my day, I couldn't wait to get home and tell my wife. In fact, I told everybody who would listen because I wanted sympathy. There is something about sharing our trials and storms that makes them feel as if they are lessened. That is why it is so incredibly burdensome when we don't feel like we have anyone who can understand our problems.

The apostles call Jesus "Teacher." They think Jesus is a great teacher; but they don't think he has the ability to influence this situation. Teachers can be incredibly helpful. They help us learn and grow and stretch our minds. Without teachers we would remain in our ignorance. Teachers perform an incredible service, but they aren't who you'd turn to in the middle of a raging sea.

In their fear and frustration, the apostles criticize Jesus' character. They ask, "Do you not care?" In that culture, disciples didn't talk to their rabbi in that way. It was a sharp rebuke but, in the face of imminent death, quite understandable. Frightened and freaking out in the middle of the storm, they lose all sense of propriety.

If you are in the middle of a storm, don't be afraid to call out to God in prayer in any way you need to, even if it might seem improper. That's better than not talking to God at all. The silent treatment is far worse than being called names.

Father Michael: Personally, as pastor, I would rather parishioners or parish staff tell me what they really think if they're angry with me. It's more helpful than keeping it to themselves, and it can lead to quicker resolution.

The narrative continues: "He woke up, rebuked the wind, and said to the sea, 'Quiet! Be still!' The wind ceased and there was great calm" (Mk 4:39). One moment the wind is raging, the waves are crashing, the boat is sinking, and the apostles are sure they're going to drown. The next, complete calm. Mark calls it a "great calm" in contrast to the great storm.

Just like that, the situation changes. Jesus doesn't have to say abracadabra or wave a magic wand. He doesn't have to invoke some long-winded prayer. He simply commands, "Quiet! Be still!" and the wind and the waves obey him. Think about it. It is one thing for the wind to die down. That happens. But the waves stop as well. Usually it takes a few minutes for waves to calm, but they obey Jesus immediately in this story.

The same Jesus who changed that situation so quickly and completely can change your situation quickly and completely. He can. If he wants to. Does he want to? We don't know. He might. Have you asked him?

> **Tom:** I was reminded of how quickly a situation can change while reflecting on this story. One of my teenage boys had been treating me very poorly. He had a nasty attitude toward me and my wife. We both prayed about it, a lot. And then one day he apologized. He came up and gave me a hug. Just like that, everything felt better. We still have stuff to work on. We still need to help him grow and mature, but just like that, the storm seemed to quiet.

Jesus quiets the storm, and then he asks the apostles, "Why are you terrified? Do you not yet have faith?" (Mk 4:40). Jesus doesn't comfort the apostles here. Instead, he challenges them for being terrified and lacking faith. The literal translation of the Greek word used here is "to lose heart." He is asking, "Why did you lose heart and not trust in my care and concern for you or ability to help you?"

Jesus didn't ask those questions because he was surprised by the apostles' lack of faith. He knew well about their lack of faith, and he headed into the storm precisely to expose them to it. He led them into that moment so they would come to know him on a whole new level.

Then Mark tells us: "They were filled with great awe and said to one another, 'Who then is this whom even wind and sea obey?'" (4:41). After witnessing these events, the apostles are forced to begin to question their view that Jesus is just another teacher. Previously, they knew he was an unequaled speaker and storyteller, a scholar of encyclopedic understanding of the Law and the prophets, a rabbi worth following. But now, their perspective is radically overturned. They are in *awe*, filled with wonder, reverence, and veneration. They are amazed at what they did not previously see.

If you are not a Christ-follower, but just picked up this book out of curiosity, we hope you will ask the same question: "Who is this man Jesus?"

Maybe you really struggle to believe this event took place, or you just don't believe it. That's very understandable. Christians themselves should reflect more on why we believe these stories. But we can all easily admit, it is amazing that two thousand years later, billions of people worship a Jewish carpenter who came from an obscure town in the backwater of the Roman empire. *Who is this man?* It is a question that generations must ask in turn and that each of us must answer for ourselves.

Jesus led the apostles into the storm. He led them into the storm so that they could come to know him better and strengthen their relationship with him. Only after going through the storm and seeing his power did they start to question whether Jesus was more than just a teacher.

Jesus wants us to wrestle with the question, *Who is he?* Who is Jesus in my life? The storms and problems into which he leads us are opportunities to see his power and presence in ways we cannot see otherwise. If we are Jesus-followers, over and over, on a daily and sometimes hourly basis, we have to remind ourselves that he is Lord of all, and that includes us. He has power and authority over everything. And we have access to him in a personal way.

Having faith in Jesus means we can turn to him in our storms, and he can calm them effectively and even immediately. Or perhaps he reverses the situation entirely. Sometimes, having faith in Jesus means believing that he is in the boat with us in the midst of the storm and allowing it, for some reason we do not appreciate at the moment.

When we hit storms, we often ask the wrong question. We ask, *Why is this happening to me?* Better questions might be:

What are you doing, God?

What do you want to teach me?

What do you want to do in this situation to help me come to stronger faith and greater trust in you?

REFLECTION QUESTIONS

1. When, if ever, have you been mad at God—perhaps when he was kind to others or because others experienced good things?

2. How has a storm or a problem helped you understand who God is in your life?

3. Are you in a storm right now? What is God teaching you in the storm?

3.

SERIOUSLY, THOSE PEOPLE ARE IN CHARGE?

When Jesus was born in Bethlehem of
Judea, in the days of King Herod, behold,
magi from the east arrived in Jerusalem,
saying, "Where is the newborn king of
the Jews? We saw his star at its rising and
have come to do him homage." When King
Herod heard this, he was greatly troubled,
and all Jerusalem with him.

—Matthew 2:1–3

I am not a crook.

—Richard Nixon

Father Michael: When I first came to this parish, there was a weekend assistant—a priest whose ministry was at a local charity during the week but who helped out here on the weekends. He usually celebrated two weekend Masses and sometimes assisted with other sacraments. We provided a stipend to him for his service but he was not actually on staff, a distinction without a difference to the average person in the pew.

He was extremely personable and friendly, even deferential to me from our first meeting, and I formed a favorable impression. Which is why, when I began to hear murmurs of criticism against him, I discounted them. But the complaints grew louder until they formed a chorus I could hardly continue to ignore. While the guy was delightful in my presence and a tremendous asset to me— given that I was the only priest here—when I wasn't around, he affected a very different demeanor. In fact, he was demanding and demeaning to staff and volunteers, and extremely unreliable when it came to showing up on time or, eventually, showing up at all. With families coming to prepare for sacraments he was very heavy-handed, and to many others, he was merely dismissive.

But the biggest problem of all came in the pulpit. He more or less used his weekend homily to demoralize parishioners. His arsenal included all the usual guilt and fear tactics, with the occasional cynical or sarcastic aside. Most people just turned

him off or avoided his Masses. But every once in
a while he could really stir things up. One particular Sunday he was describing a recent fundraiser
the parish had hosted that was unsuccessful. As
I stuck my head out of the sacristy, I could hear
him saying, with a raised voice, "Shame on you,
shame on you!" More than a few people got up
and walked out. (Just for your information, shortly
after that memorable day Father found another
weekend engagement, and we parted company.)

No matter who you are, you have probably experienced a
situation in which you or a loved one struggled under the
authority of someone who abused their power. Rather than
using their authority in service to the common good, they
used it for heavy-handed or self-centered purposes, dimin-
ishing the quality of life of others.

Maybe it is a coach who makes your life miserable. His
kid gets all the playing time—despite not being very good—
while your child rides the bench. Or maybe it is someone in
your homeowners' association. They are drunk with power,
lording over everyone else, tirelessly on the lookout for the
slightest infraction of the neighborhood covenant. It makes
you so mad you want to move.

It could be a problem at work. Your boss is angry and
arrogant. Or you have seen how the senior leadership of
your company, who won't listen to anyone and refuse to
consider desperately needed new ideas, are driving away the
very best talent in the organization.

Perhaps, no matter your political leanings, you have felt frustrated by the other party being in power or disappointed by leaders you thought were more principled when they caved to the pressures around them.

And then there is the Church. How does God allow people who abuse their authority to stay in power in the Church? Of all places, we would think the realm of religion should be free of abuses of power and authority. This is especially heartbreaking to us. People leave the Church because leaders drive them away. We look around and see poor religious leaders and wonder why God doesn't do something.

In recent years we have learned of sickening corruption among members of the clergy, religious sisters, theologians, and lay Catholic leaders, but this isn't a new problem. At his coronation, Napoleon famously snatched the crown away from the pope in order to crown himself emperor of the French. Later, the two purportedly had a sharp exchange in which Napoleon railed, "I will destroy this Church of yours!" To which Pius VII coolly replied, "If the clergy have not accomplished that themselves in over 1,800 years, how can you hope to succeed?"

Why does God allow people who are corrupt or unjust to remain in charge? Why does he permit people who abuse their power or who are just plain incompetent to rule? This is a recurring theme throughout the scriptures, especially in the Old Testament. If God was in charge and the nation of Israel was his chosen nation, why does he allow powerful kings to rise up in opposition to Israel, even seeking its complete annihilation?

We forget sometimes that the scriptures are set in history with people who faced ordinary, everyday problems as well as global, geopolitical ones. The Israelites lived in the shadow of the most powerful armies and nations of the time. Those nations used their power to dominate and oppress weaker nations.

Israel's struggles form the backdrop to many of the stories we read. The Bible, which covers roughly two millennia of history, describes Israel successively contending with the Egyptians, Assyrians, Babylonians, Persians, Greeks, and Romans. They were fierce enemies who brought cruel overlords: the kings of Assyria, the pharaohs of Egypt, the emperors of Rome.

If God is all-powerful and all-knowing, why did he permit those people to be in charge and to mock the true ruler of the earth? Their oppressive rule seems to belie his power. The people of Israel wrestled with this question. The human authors of scripture had to address these issues under the inspiration of the Holy Spirit. Without God's revelation, they couldn't make sense of it either.

A BAD KING

There are numerous scriptures we could use to examine this topic. We are going to look at a passage from the book of Daniel to help us make sense of what God is doing when the wrong people rule.

The book of Daniel is set about six hundred years before Christ. In the year 587, the Babylonians laid siege to Jerusalem, completely destroying it and devastating its people.

Certainly the biggest blow to the city and its inhabitants was the destruction of the Temple. And not only did the Babylonians destroy the Temple, but they also killed King Zedekiah's sons in front of him, then gouged out his eyes so that their deaths were the last things he ever saw. That was typical of the brutality of the Babylonians. But Zedekiah had provoked this response by attempting an ill-conceived rebellion against the far more powerful imperial force.

After conquering a city, the Babylonians would send many of its citizens into exile to further solidify their power. Nebuchadnezzar, the king of Babylon, always took the best and brightest people among the aristocracy and ruling class he had conquered to serve in various capacities at his court. Among those taken from Judah was a young nobleman named Daniel. The book of Daniel tells his story as well as that of other Jewish exiles. The main theme of the book is how Jews in exile still honored God despite living in a culture that was entirely hostile to their faith.

Daniel leaves Jerusalem as a young man. However, the story we are looking at takes place later in his life when Daniel has risen to the role of senior statesman. But our story does not begin with Daniel; it begins with a king who succeeded Nebuchadnezzar. His name was Belshazzar.

At a certain point, Belshazzar throws a lavish party in Babylon for the nobles and higher-ups at court. Actually, the "party" is an orgy of debauchery and blasphemy, the latter of which gets them into some trouble. Before the Babylonians destroyed the Jerusalem Temple, they had taken all the ceremonial vessels, used to worship and honor the living God, as trophies for having conquered the city.

The book of Daniel tells us, "Under the influence of the wine, [Belshazzar] ordered the gold and silver vessels which Nebuchadnezzar, his father, had taken from the temple in Jerusalem, to be brought in so that the king, his nobles, his consorts, and his concubines might drink from them" (Dn 5:2). So Belshazzar, drunk with wine, proceeds to enhance his bacchanal with brazen sacrilege. He calls for the sacred vessels his father had looted from the Temple and proceeds to desecrate them as props for his party. In the process, he and his fellow revelers profane the God of Israel, a decadent act of iconoclasm and idolatry.

They drink their wine from the Temple cups and praise their gods for giving them victory over the God of Israel. But while they are drinking, something happens. "Suddenly, opposite the lampstand, the fingers of a human hand appeared, writing on the plaster of the wall in the king's palace" (Dn 5:5). You have probably heard the expression, "The handwriting is on the wall." It is a striking scene, a disembodied hand appearing to deliver a message: "When the king saw the hand that wrote, his face became pale; his thoughts terrified him, his hip joints shook, and his knees knocked" (Dn 5:5–6).

To say the least, the party was over. The king is terrified, even though he hardly understands what is happening or what it might mean. He urgently calls for an interpretation of this wondrous sign and promises rich rewards for anyone who can do it. Enter Daniel, who was known at the court as a visionary and prophet. Daniel tells the king, "You may keep your gifts, or give your presents to someone else; but the writing I will read for the king, and tell what it means" (Dn 5:17).

Daniel rejects the king's gifts but promises to interpret the sign. However, before Daniel answers Belshazzar, he reminds him of an event that the king knew well:

> The Most High God gave your father Nebuchadnezzar kingship, greatness, splendor, and majesty. . . . But when his heart became proud and his spirit hardened by insolence, he was put down from his royal throne and deprived of his glory; he was cast out from human society and his heart was made like that of a beast; he lived with wild asses, and ate grass like an ox; his body was bathed with the dew of heaven, until he learned that the Most High God is sovereign over human kingship and sets over it whom he will. (Dn 5:18, 20–21)

The event is told in an earlier chapter of Daniel. Nebuchadnezzar ruled the world, but he became so proud that for a time he actually went mad. He acted like a wild animal, eating grass and sleeping outdoors. Perhaps he was suffering from a real, though rare, mental illness known as boanthropy, which causes its victims to imitate the behavior of cattle. Nebuchadnezzar continued to descend into madness until he learned that he was *not* the most powerful being in the universe. He came to see that the Most High God is sovereign over all the kings of the earth. He realized that he only ruled because God allowed him to.

Admittedly those verses might raise more questions than they answer. Stay with us, though; it all adds up. Daniel continues, "You, his son, Belshazzar, have not humbled your heart, though you knew all this; you have rebelled against the Lord of heaven" (Dn 5:22–23). Daniel tells Belshazzar that in drinking from the Temple vessels, he has now crossed a line. He has gone too far, repeating and doubling his father's sacrilege. Belshazzar knew what had happened to Nebuchadnezzar, but he mocked God anyway.

Daniel describes the message written by the disembodied hand: "This is the writing that was inscribed: MENE, TEKEL, and PERES" (Dn 5:25). They were words of measurement. They don't mean much to us, and on the surface they didn't mean much to the king and his nobles, either. So Daniel goes on to this interpretation of the matter: "MENE, God has numbered your kingdom and put an end to it; TEKEL, you have been weighed on the scales and found wanting; PERES, your kingdom has been divided and given to the Medes and Persians" (Dn 5:26–28).

Mene—Unbeknownst to Belshazzar, God had numbered his days. He had authority only for a limited amount of time, and that time was up. His reign was coming to an end.

Tekel—God has placed Belshazzar's reign under judgment and found it lacking.

Peres—Since Belshazzar had failed to meet God's expectations, he was being deposed and his kingdom divided among the Medes and Persians. God in his wisdom had determined that now was the time for Belshazzar to lose his power. The kingdom would be taken away from him.

The story concludes: "That very night Belshazzar, the Chaldean king, was slain: And Darius the Mede succeeded to the kingdom" (Dn 5:30–6:1).

We know from history that Babylon had been under assault. Belshazzar was ruling with a false sense of security, knowing that the Persian army could not breach the city walls. It is true that Babylon's walls were impenetrable. They couldn't be breached, and they couldn't be scaled. But the Persian engineers discovered an ingenious way to go *under* the walls. And since the walls were unguarded, the Persians, once inside the city, conquered it without a fight.

BAD RELIGIOUS LEADERS

Let us return again to the issue of corruption and poor leaders in the Church. While it is disappointing to see self-centered leadership in the world, we feel it even more acutely when it comes to religion. We assume that God would surely preserve and protect the community of faith from selfish leaders. But, of course, such is not the case.

We know from history, both ancient and contemporary, that plenty of people have used their ecclesial office for self-serving purposes and corrupt ends. Even a superficial survey would list many examples, reaching from the most provincial parish to the corridors of the Vatican. It scandalizes, angers, and saddens all of us and moves many people to walk away from the Church and even God. The faith of more than a few has been destroyed, with some people developing a scarred view of God himself. Why does God allow such evil even in his Church?

Let's make one point clear. While God permits leaders to choose corruption, nothing angers him more than the abuse of religious authority. Nothing. If you want to make God mad, then abuse religious power and authority. Use God to oppress and control others. Use God and his name to get what you want. Use God and religion to gain power, pleasure, prestige, or possessions rather than to serve people, and you make God very, very angry.

Nothing angers God more. How do we know that? Throughout the gospels, we see how angry it made Jesus. Just as the power of other nations forms the backdrop of much of the Old Testament, Jesus' confrontation with people in religious authority serves as a motif of the gospels. And that theme continues in the Acts of the Apostles.

Jesus confronted the abuse of religious authority more directly and more vigorously than anything else. In fact, he reserved his most scathing criticism not for tax collectors, prostitutes, and other sinners but for the scribes, Pharisees, Sadducees, and other religious leaders. He considered them a "brood of vipers" (dangerous and deadly; Mt 12:34) and "whitewashed tombs" (filled with death and decay; Mt 23:27). He called them "blind guides" (Mt 15:14), "blind fools" (Mt 23:17), and, most often, simply "hypocrites" (Mt 23:23 and elsewhere). Read through Matthew 23 if you want to see how angry he could get. Jesus excoriated the religious leaders.

Just as Daniel told Belshazzar that his use of power was being evaluated and found wanting, Jesus confronted the religious leaders with the same judgment. And just as Daniel told Belshazzar that his power and authority were coming to an end, so Jesus relayed the same message to the religious leaders of his time. Jesus most explicitly confronts them in a parable that we find in the Gospel of Matthew.

Jesus tells the parable after his triumphant entry into Jerusalem on Palm Sunday. Jesus parades into Jerusalem, the home turf of the religious leaders, like a rock star. He had recently raised Lazarus from the dead. Throughout his public ministry, he very skillfully kept a lid on unfolding events and the public response to buy the time he needed to accomplish his mission. But with the raising of Lazarus, he purposefully and powerfully sets in motion the cataclysmic events that would inexorably and immediately lead to Calvary. The crowds are cheering him as a conquering king; the Jewish leaders consider him an illegitimate claimant to their authority. Regarding his popularity, they are apoplectic with jealousy.

Jesus goes to the Temple, where he aggressively invites conflict, overturning the money changers' tables and expelling the merchants from the sacred precincts. Then he wades into controversy, disputing with not one but all of the various political and religious factions of the day: the Pharisees, the Sadducees, and the Herodians. Usually in conflict with one another, they are here united by a common enemy: Jesus. They hate him.

Why? Because he's taken their playbook for how to approach God and just thrown it out. And to make matters worse, he's successful. People were drawn to him because he loved and served them. He made a relationship with God accessible to the average person. The lost, the "unchurched," were attracted to him because he gave their lives meaning and direction. He told people that their lives mattered.

Jesus succeeds in attracting people, while the religious leaders had only alienated the crowds. The religious leaders, who should have been caring for and growing God's family, instead made it daunting and difficult to live faithfully as a religious Jew. Most ordinary people simply walked away and gave up trying. The rules were so confusing and complex that nobody could follow them. The leaders themselves couldn't obey them; they hypocritically absented themselves from many of the laws they tried to impose on everyone else.

At this point the religious leaders are enraged at everything that is happening and are looking for blood. That was the scene in the week we call holy. So, in the midst of this alarming scenario, what does Jesus do? He tells a story: "There was a landowner who planted a vineyard, put a hedge around it, dug a wine press in it, and built a tower. Then he leased it to tenants and went on a journey" (Mt 21:33). This was something a businessman or entrepreneur of that time would do. First, the owner determined that a property was suitable for cultivation as a vineyard. Then he undertook the work of getting the vineyard going and establishing the necessary infrastructure to keep it going.

- He plants the vineyard, an obvious step.
- He puts up a hedge and builds a tower, to keep out wild animals and thieves who might damage, destroy, or steal his harvest.
- He digs a wine press, a basin carved out of stone in which grapes were crushed; the grape juice flowed out of the drains in the press into vats where it fermented into wine.

Then the landowner rents the vineyard to farmers to tend the vines and produce fruit. This was a typical business arrangement in that region in the first century. Nonresidential landowners would contract with local peasants, who might otherwise be destitute, having no land of their own. They work for him and get to share in the profits. But the profit, in this case the fruit of the vine, belongs to the landowner. Jesus continues: "When vintage time drew near, he sent his servants to the tenants to obtain his produce. But the tenants seized the servants and one they beat, another they killed, and a third they stoned. Again he sent other servants, more numerous than the first ones, but they treated them in the same way" (Mt 21:34–36).

This is outrageous. The landowner seeks what already belongs to him, the fruit of the vineyard that he planted. And these people, who are supposed to be serving him, withhold from him his fruit. Then it gets worse; the guy sends his son. "But when the tenants saw the son, they said to one another, 'This is the heir. Come, let us kill him and acquire his inheritance.' They seized him, threw him out of the vineyard, and killed him" (Mt 21:38–39).

Father Michael: So this is crazy. It is a crazy story. How many times have I read the gospel at Mass, and it's completely crazy? And nobody blinks. No one seems to notice. And I feel like shouting, "Did you just hear what I read? It is absolutely crazy. This is jaw-droppingly absurd. Hello, is anyone listening? They killed him. They killed him thinking they would get the property if they did so." Insane story.

Anyway, we know that in Jesus' parables each character represents someone. Someone, for instance, usually represents God, and in this parable that is the owner of the vineyard. That would mean that Jesus is the landowner's son—the one who is killed. The tenants? That would doubtless be, as Matthew later tells us, the religious leaders to whom Jesus is telling the story. But Jesus' storytelling is so masterful that they're caught up in the narrative, failing to recognize themselves in the story.

So Jesus asks the religious leaders, "What will the owner of the vineyard do to those tenants when he comes?" (Mt 21:40). With moral outrage and indignation at the very idea of this injustice and breach of the established social order, they do not hesitate to answer: "He will put those wretched men to a wretched death and lease his vineyard to other tenants who will give him the produce at the proper times" (Mt 21:41). Now here comes the lesson. Jesus says to them, "Did you never read in the scriptures: 'The stone that the builders rejected has become the cornerstone; by the Lord has this been done, and it is wonderful in our eyes'?" (Mt 21:42, quoting Ps 118:22–23).

Jesus tells the leaders that the Messiah, their long-awaited Savior, is to be rejected by the religious establishment but will become the cornerstone for the new movement God is building. Then Jesus lowers the boom. He says to the chief priests and elders, "Therefore, I say to you, the kingdom of God will be taken away from you and given to a people that will produce its fruit" (Mt 21:43). Jesus constantly talks about God's kingdom in his parables. In fact, the kingdom is the central topic of his parables. God's kingdom is the place where God reigns. It is where God's will is done. The kingdom of God will be taken away from them and given to people who will produce its fruit.

What does it mean to produce the *fruit* of God's kingdom? We'll return to the scripture in a moment. But before we get there, let's acknowledge that another word we could use for *fruit* would be *success*. Just as Jesus' success and popularity were offensive to the religious leaders, they are often offensive to churchpeople in churchworld.

We've heard churchpeople, in the wake of dull efforts and dismal failures, quote St. Teresa of Calcutta: "God didn't call me to be successful. He called me to be faithful." But maybe she wasn't talking primarily about embracing failure. Maybe she was emphasizing obedient service. In her case (you'd have to admit), she was singularly *successful*. In fact, Mother Teresa stands among the most successful and innovative Church leaders of the twentieth century, founding one of the fastest-growing religious orders in the world. Maybe she understood something churchpeople forget or just get wrong. God calls us to faithful service, and when we provide it, he provides the success, he brings the fruit.

Scripture makes it clear that God expects us to be faithful *and* fruitful. Obedience doesn't preclude fruit; it *necessitates it*. So what does it mean to be fruitful? Let's return to the scriptures. Except this time, let's jump ahead in the story to look at the Acts of the Apostles.

What has happened since the last scene? The kingdom of God is being taken away from the Pharisees and other religious leaders and given to a people who will produce its fruit. The Acts of the Apostles tells us about the transfer of power. The kingdom is given to a new movement led by ordinary, uneducated fishermen that Jesus calls the *Church*. Ultimately, that transfer of power was complete in AD 70 when the Romans destroyed the second Temple that was never rebuilt. But even before its ultimate destruction, Temple worship was in decline while the Church was growing exponentially.

Over and over again, the Acts of the Apostles tells about the growth of that movement. The Church grew and grew and grew. Check out these verses:

> Those who accepted his message were baptized, and about three thousand persons were **added** that day. (Acts 2:41)

> And every day the Lord **added to their number** those who were being saved. (Acts 2:47)

> The word of God continued to spread; and the number of disciples in Jerusalem **increased** greatly. (Acts 6:7)

The church throughout all Judea, Galilee, and Samaria
was at peace. It was being built up and walked in the fear
of the Lord, and with the consolation of the holy Spirit it
grew in numbers. (Acts 9:31)

Notice a pattern here? This is the Church in its earliest, pur-
est, and most exuberant form. This is the Church as Jesus
intended it to be. You cannot read the Acts of the Apostles
and not see success. And success is measured in growth: the
Early Church grew *wider*. The Church also grew *deeper* as
people became more and more committed to a relationship
with Jesus Christ. They sacrificed their time, their energy,
and their finances to follow Jesus and live according to his
teaching and example.

God wants his Church to grow *wider and deeper*. It seems
odd to have to argue that, but evidently it's not obvious at
all. So we'll say it: God wants us to grow. God's fruit is his
people. Like Jesus, the Church is charged to attract people
who are considered far from God. Our first job is to bring
them into a relationship with his Son. Next, we help them
grow as fully devoted followers of Jesus Christ. Then it's all
about enlisting their help in doing the same for others.

The Church is not a building. Nor is it a reference to religious leaders and church workers. The Church is everyone
who follows Jesus. It exists to bring others into a relationship with the Lord. In every generation, there is corruption
and misuse of power in the Church. But, in every generation
God raises up new leaders who will produce more fruit.

Not everything that happens on this earth is God's will.
Some people come to power despite God's will. God gives

us freedom, and if we choose bad leaders or create systems that allow poor leaders to rise to the top, that's not on God, that's on us—our choices and our decisions. God respects our free will enough to let us exercise it. The book of Samuel tells us that the nation of Israel demanded to have a king. But God didn't want them to have a king because he knew it would lead to higher taxes and make their lives more challenging in other ways. He knew it would introduce all kinds of unnecessary pain. However, eventually he relented. He respected their free will. They got their king (and higher taxes). We choose bad leaders, and God lets us.

We also have to acknowledge that God doesn't have a lot to work with. The problem is fallen human nature. People are notoriously bad at handling power well; they use the position to serve themselves. It is said, "Power tends to corrupt, and absolute power corrupts absolutely."

Tom: If you think about it, you have probably used authority in the wrong way too. I know as a parent I have. There are times when I have thought of myself before my kids. I have been self-centered and gotten mad at them rather than using my authority over them for their good. Before I had children, seeing parents yelling at their kids in a grocery store or elsewhere in public, I would shake my head in disapproval, thinking, *What a bad parent.* Now, if I am out and about and see a parent yelling at a child, I shake my head and think, *I've been there.* I was a much better father before I had kids!

If you are a manager or supervisor, you know you haven't been perfect in the use of your authority. You haven't always used your power and position for others.

In our culture, we question the abuse of power by self-centered leaders, but the ancient world accepted that as a fact of life. After all, that was precisely why anyone would have sought power. In Mark's gospel, Jesus comments, "You know that those who are recognized as rulers over the Gentiles lord it over them, and their great ones make their authority over them felt" (10:42). The apostles were probably thinking, *Yes, that's why we can't wait until you are in charge, Jesus. We are looking forward to the day when we can tell other people what to do.* Jesus taught differently.

He said to them, "But it shall not be so among you. Rather, whoever wishes to be great among you will be your servant; whoever wishes to be first among you will be the slave of all. For the Son of Man did not come to be served but to serve and to give his life as a ransom for many" (Mk 10:43–45). Jesus had to teach his earliest friends and followers to use their authority and influence for others instead of for themselves. It was his teaching that totally reversed how we view leadership. As Christ-followers, we believe authority and power should be used to serve people and not for personal gain.

It is normal to question why God allows the wrong people to rule. But abuse of power can also serve as a reminder to seek God's grace in the exercise of our own influence. We can become the type of people who embrace the kingdom of God and bear its fruit, by being servants of others.

God's kingdom is coming. One day he will fully and completely establish his kingdom on earth as it is in heaven. We often think of eternity as a very passive experience, but that is not how Jesus presents it. For him it is precisely a matter of power and authority. How well we use the power and authority given to us in this world will affect our position in the next. Here is the great irony: the people who wield power in this world only for themselves eventually become powerless. Control freaks ultimately always lose control. The Most High God is sovereign, *and* he allows free will. Only people who choose to align their will with his, using their power and influence to love and serve others, will rule. People who have used their power and influence to love and serve others will rule.

So why does God allow the wrong people to remain in charge? Remember that Belshazzar at the height of his royal reign and the Pharisees presiding in the splendor of the Temple were already under God's judgment. It might seem like nothing is happening, but that is simply not the case. God is developing the ends and outcomes he desires.

REFLECTION QUESTIONS

1. When have you been frustrated by someone in power?

2. Why do you think God allows the wrong people to stay in power?

3. How well do you handle authority? What can you do to handle it in a way that better serves others?

4.

SERIOUSLY, YOU'RE IN MY WAY

Consider it all joy, my brothers, when you encounter various trials, for you know that the testing of your faith produces perseverance. And let perseverance be perfect, so that you may be perfect and complete, lacking in nothing.

—James 1:2–4

It's not that I'm so smart, it's just that I stay with problems longer.

—Albert Einstein

Father Michael: As a first-time pastor, I was ignorant about many things. And, as a result, I consistently made problems for myself. My first summer,

I decided to paint the entry area of the parish office. It needed painting, and I thought it would be a good summertime project. There were pictures in the hallway that had been placed there by the former pastor. We took them down to paint and subsequently rehung them . . . but in a different order. This sparked such a negative reaction that I eventually received a visit from the bishop.

Another time, I tried to organize a fundraiser to send the youth group to World Youth Day. A local car dealer sold us a new car at a considerable discount, and we proceeded to sell raffle tickets. The only problem was, we didn't sell enough to even cover the cost of the car, so we had to keep extending the drawing . . . and extending the drawing. All the while the car sat in front of the church as a great big shining reminder of my failed attempt at fundraising.

But far and away my biggest blunder in those early years was a real rookie move. I somewhat cavalierly changed the time of daily Mass. It never occurred to me that anyone would have strong opinions about something as deeply inconsequential as the time of daily Mass—especially considering the dozen or so Masses available at neighboring parishes nearly every day of the week. No big deal, right? Boy oh boy, was I wrong. Pretty much all hell broke loose. Letters to the bishop denouncing me, letters to me denouncing me, tears, jeers, you name it. In my naïveté I was

especially troubled as people threatened to withhold their contributions and even leave the parish
entirely. How, I wondered, could this be happening in a Catholic church? How could this be happening to *me*? I came to the parish to serve the
Lord, and he didn't seem to be on my side.

Let's face it, there are times when God seems uncooperative. There are even times when it looks like God is deliberately making life difficult. We think that if God would just
remove the obstacles in our way, then life would be much
better or at least easier.

- Maybe for you there is an obstacle in your professional
  life. Your contributions at work haven't been appreci-
  ated and you haven't moved up in your organization as
  you expected. You're unsure what to do.
- Maybe you feel that you and your spouse would have a
  better marriage if your in-laws minded their own business instead of constantly getting into the mix. And
  then there's that one thorny issue that you both keep
  stumbling over but that you just can't seem to resolve.
- Your issue may be health related. You are constantly
  dealing with chronic pain or some disability or disease,
  and if you weren't sick you could accomplish so much
  more. And yet no matter what you do, your health does
  not improve.
- Money could be the problem that won't go away for
  you. You work hard; you try to save; but you seem to go
  nowhere.

- Maybe it's loneliness. You try to make friends; you're generous and kind to people; you're a good person; but you feel all alone and on your own.
- Or maybe it all comes down to worry. You can't make even simple decisions without being plagued by worry.

Obstacles such as these feel like roadblocks and keep us from getting anywhere. While others seem to fly along effortlessly, we keep stumbling. And God permits it? God wills it? At the very least, it seems that God allows obstacles to get in our way. Why? Let us at least reassure you that it's not just you, and you're not the first.

THE THIRSTY CROWD

The second book of the Bible is called Exodus. Exodus tells the story of the Israelites' escape from slavery in Egypt. God sees the suffering of his people and sends Moses to challenge the Egyptian pharaoh to let his people go. The pharaoh refuses, and so God sends ten plagues that more or less force him to relent. The pharaoh permits the Israelites to leave Egypt, but then he has a change of heart and unleashes his army, to hunt the Israelites down and bring them back. As the Israelites approach the Red Sea, the Egyptian forces, the most powerful in the world at the time, close in on them from behind. They're trapped.

It must have been a real *Where is God?* kind of moment for Moses. After all, it was God's idea to leave Egypt. But instead of complaining, as *we* might be tempted to do, Moses prays. God responds with the incredible miracle of the parting of the Red Sea. The Israelites then begin their journey to the Promised Land—a land where they will eventually settle in peace and prosperity.

It is a journey that should have taken only about eleven days. All is going great. So great, the Israelites promptly forget all about God. As a result, their sprint to the "land of milk and honey" turns into a marathon of forty years filled with challenges like this episode we read about in chapter 17: "From the wilderness of Sin the whole Israelite community journeyed by stages, as the LORD directed, and encamped at Rephidim. But there was no water for the people to drink" (Ex 17:1). Here the Israelites are, following the instructions of the Lord, but the results are disappointing, even dangerous. They are in need of water and expect that the Lord is leading them to it. But it's not there.

You know that feeling. You are tired after a rough day at work, but you get home and the house is in disarray and the kids are quarreling. To say the least, it's not the environment you were looking forward to. Or you come to the end of a long journey, and all you want to do is take a shower and get to bed, but the hotel room isn't ready. And in that moment it is very difficult to take the disappointment graciously. You might do what the Israelites did. "And so they quarreled with Moses and said, 'Give us water to drink.' Moses replied to them, 'Why do you quarrel with me? Why do you put the LORD to a test?'" (Ex 17:2).

Whenever we have a problem, we want to find someone to blame. The people find fault with Moses and blame him for their lack of water. They become demanding, and in

their disappointment they develop a hardness of heart. They
want what they want, and they want it now!

> **Father Michael:** We have experienced this in the
> life of the parish on many occasions. For instance,
> when we first came to the parish, the music pro-
> gram we inherited was a problem. The problem,
> simply stated, was that nobody liked the music.
> After enduring myriad complaints, as well as our
> own disappointment with the program, we finally
> worked our way into a position to hire a profes-
> sional music director. I was so excited on his first
> weekend that I positioned myself by the front
> door to greet exiting parishioners and enjoy their
> accolades. It was not to be. I'll never forget the
> comment from the very first lady coming out of
> church: "That young man is far too loud. Tell him
> to tone it down." A chorus of complaints followed,
> including one man's suggestion that we forgo
> the music program entirely and just have "quiet"
> Masses. What a disappointment! I guess I know
> how Moses felt.

At other times, we've been the ones grumbling and complaining. We both can easily see how God has been faithful
in helping us rebuild our parish and grow it into a healthy
community of faith. Over and over again he has provided
the necessary resources to expand our facility and build our
programs and services. And yet if we are entirely honest
with ourselves, we must admit that the moment we meet any

disappointment, we can often be like those Israelites grumbling in the desert. We can forget about God's past faithfulness. We can have an attitude of *What have you done for us lately, God?* It seems pretty arrogant, doesn't it, to have that kind of attitude toward the Almighty, the Maker of heaven and earth? But we are all guilty of it.

In those times, we would do well to remind ourselves, or allow others to remind us, of God's faithfulness. This is what Moses does. He pushes back on the Israelites and tells them to remember all the things God has already done for them. And if God has provided in the past, of course he will provide for them moving forward, so they can relax and not worry. But the people don't accept Moses's reassurances. Instead their complaining intensifies: "In their thirst for water, the people grumbled against Moses, saying, 'Why then did you bring us up out of Egypt? To have us die of thirst with our children and our livestock?'" (Ex 17:3). They become more and more agitated and outspoken, even accusing Moses of plotting murder. That is some kind of grumbling.

Grumbling comes from ingratitude. It is choosing to be disgruntled in the face of discomfort, difficulties, or disappointments. Grumbling also stems from distrust; here, distrust of Moses, for sure, but ultimately distrust of God. This can be a very dangerous attitude of the heart. If we are not careful, it can become a self-defeating habit whenever we face difficulties or challenges.

"So Moses cried out to the Lord, 'What shall I do with this people? A little more and they will stone me!'" (Ex

17:4). There is a big difference between Moses's reaction to a difficult situation and that of the people of Israel. While the people complain *against* and *about* God and question his character, Moses complains *to* God and asks him for direction.

There is all the difference in the world between complaining *about* someone to another person and complaining *to* them. When you complain about someone, you aren't addressing the problem with them. Murmuring about your spouse won't fix your marriage. Grumbling about your kids' irresponsibility won't help them learn to be responsible. Griping about your coworker or boss won't help them do a better job, and it won't be of any help to you either. Neither does it show respect for the relationship.

This does not mean you can never share the problems you are having with a third party in a discreet, confidential manner. Seeking advice on how to interact with someone makes sense and can be helpful. But the motivation is very important.

Tom: One of my coworkers at the parish was giving us a great deal of pushback about some staff changes Michael and I wanted to make. It seemed so unnecessary and unfair that I found myself resenting him, or at least his attitude. Ironically, as I was writing this chapter about not grumbling and complaining, I took a break to complain about him to my wife. But I stopped myself, realizing that if I didn't address the problem with my coworker directly, our relationship would suffer and I would

be missing out on a golden opportunity to coach
him on becoming a more effective teammate.

If we respect the relationship and the person, if we seek positive change, we will bring challenges *to them*. Relationships
become stronger when we actually address our problems,
and that includes our relationship with God. When you
feel like God is not helping you out or is letting you down,
allowing you to experience difficult situations, you can
tell him that you are frustrated. You can complain to him.
Being honest with God about your feelings will strengthen
your relationship with him.

Moses complained *to* God, not *about* him. Since he
addressed God directly, he received a direct response: "The
LORD answered Moses: Go on ahead of the people, and take
along with you some of the elders of Israel, holding in your
hand, as you go, the staff with which you struck the Nile.
I will be standing there before you on the rock in Horeb.
Strike the rock, and the water will flow from it for the people to drink. Moses did this, in the sight of the elders of
Israel" (Ex 17:5–6). Moses complained to God, and God
answered. He told Moses to take up the rod he had used to
initiate the plagues in Egypt and to part the Red Sea. The
rod was a sign of Moses's authority. It also stood as a symbol
of his dependence on God in direct contrast to the people's
grumbling and complaining. He would use this rod to draw
water from a rock.

God told Moses to leave the camp because, by their
grumbling, the people had forfeited the right to see God
provide. In fact, their grumbling was getting in the way of

God's acting on their behalf. God wants to partner with us in bringing good things into our lives, our families, our world. But our complaints block his activity. Be very aware of the words you use in your life. Our *words* create our *worlds*. Your words create the experience and shape the environment at home, at work, with family and friends. Grumbling and complaining create a world that blocks out God's love and grace. They keep us from seeing this love and grace at work.

"The place was named Massah and Meribah, because the Israelites quarreled there and tested the LORD, saying, 'Is the LORD in our midst or not?'" (Ex 17:7). Moses obeyed, and God responded. But even though God provided water and the Israelites got what they wanted, their relationship was damaged. Moses therefore named the place Massah and Meribah. *Massah* means "testing." God was giving the Israelites a test—a test they had failed earlier. We can read about it in previous chapters of Exodus. They failed to trust in God when they were threatened by the Egyptian army. Yet God delivered them. They failed to trust when there didn't seem to be any food in the desert. Yet God fed them.

So God gave them another opportunity to trust him with a lack of water, and they failed again. Each time they faced a challenge, they failed to trust. In fact, rather than passing the test, they actually tested God, as if he needed to prove himself all over again. They acted as though they were God's judge instead of God's judgeship over them. As a result, that entire generation of Israelites denied themselves the sight of the Promised Land. A journey that should have taken eleven days stretched out over forty years because of the Israelites' refusal to put away their doubt and division. This is why the place was renamed Meribah, which means "quarreling."

God allows difficulties in our life to test us. God tries our character in order to strengthen and improve it. God tries and tests us so that we will choose to grow into people who trust him no matter the externals of our situation. In the process, we learn lessons that can only be learned in the laboratory of life.

Possibly you experience obstacles over and over again because God wants to bring you to a different place, a deeper level of trust in him. God never appears to someone in the Bible and says, "I have a really easy job for you, and I promise to smooth out even the smallest obstacles." Nothing worth accomplishing is ever easy; it never comes without difficulties.

Obstacles force us to lean into God. If we are willing to trust him and depend on his grace, we will see his power as Moses did. But if we choose to grumble and complain, we will miss his power. God's grace works through human weakness when weak humans choose to trust him.

God isn't interested in making your life easier. God isn't interested in making your life more comfortable. That's often *our* goal, but not God's. God does want to give you rest. God does want you to live in joy. God can bring you comfort and grant you peace. But there are no times in scripture when Jesus teaches, "And when you pray, say, 'Heavenly Father, make my life easy and comfortable.'" Do the search; it isn't in there.

There are certainly some toxic situations you should avoid. We're not saying you should remain in any abusive circumstances; of course God does not desire that. But be careful of fleeing a situation just because it is difficult. Some people go from company to company, job to job, friendship to friendship, marriage to marriage, church to church because when the going gets tough, they run.

God's goal is to teach us to rely on him and his grace so that we can become the person he created us to be. God's goal is for us to come to know our need for him in every area of our life. God's goal is to sharpen and transform our character into his Son's.

Maybe God *is* getting in your way because there is something he is trying to teach you. Maybe you keep having the same problem because God wants you to learn something new about him or about how to treat people. God was trying to teach the Israelites that he was trustworthy. He kept putting them in positions where they had to depend on him to meet their needs and rely on his grace. He had to do it over and over again because they weren't getting the lesson, even after he proved faithful.

So, what obstacle do you keep coming up against? Instead of grumbling and complaining about the problem, bring it to God. Ask him what he wants you to learn from the situation. Ask him how it can teach you to depend on his grace.

THE HUNGRY CROWD

Sometimes God allows difficulties so we will grow to trust him. However, there is another reason God will lead us into difficult situations, as we discover in the sixth chapter of the Gospel of Mark. Here the apostles return to Jesus after undertaking a mission of preaching and teaching. The gospel tells us that they are so inundated with followers that they don't even have a chance to eat. They need a break, and Jesus knows it. Maybe you can relate to that feeling.

Jesus says, "Come away by yourselves to a deserted place and rest a while" (Mk 6:31). That's the plan. So they get in a boat to escape the crowds. But when Jesus "disembarked and saw the vast crowd, his heart was moved with pity for them, for they were like sheep without a shepherd; and he began to teach them many things" (Mk 6:34). The plan changes because the crowds follow Jesus. Have you noticed how often in the scriptures Jesus is surrounded by crowds? People wanted to be around him. They liked him. Think about that. People who were nothing like him liked him. They found him engaging, and his Church should be engaging too.

This episode is related in all four gospels. And from the other accounts we know that, in fact, the crowd that greeted Jesus on the opposite shore was the same one he had just left—on the other side. Sometimes a problem not only gets in your way but actually follows you around. The people that the apostles are trying to avoid run ahead of them to the other side of the Sea of Galilee and beat them there. This large, enthusiastic crowd is eager to hear more from Jesus.

The gathering was probably a lot like a modern-day political rally. In that area of the world, at that time, there was great messianic fervor. People were looking for someone to lead them to overthrow the despised Roman occupiers. From the Gospel of John, we know that this crowd tries to make Jesus king. This group was looking to raise up a revolutionary leader, and they thought Jesus might be their man. But Jesus knows that no earthly king can solve their problems.

The crowd is disappointed in Jesus' unwillingness to be their political figurehead. But Jesus has compassion for them because they are leaderless. He takes time to teach them even though Mark tells us it is getting late. And that's making the apostles a bit nervous, so they go to Jesus and say, "This is a deserted place and it is already very late. Dismiss them so that they can go to the surrounding farms and villages and buy themselves something to eat" (Mk 6:35–36).

The sun is going down. They are in the middle of nowhere. They've got five thousand hungry and tired people on their hands. In other words, they've got a problem. Besides, the apostles probably feared the politically motivated crowd could become a mob, so dispersing them made sense. They see a problem, or a number of problems, and they bring Jesus a solution. Let the people go home, go find food, or just go. It is so easy. It is such an easy solution.

Have you ever gone to your boss in the midst of a problem with an easy solution? It seems completely reasonable to you, and it will make everyone's life easier. But your boss says no and, in fact, gives you *more* work to do. That's what

Jesus does here. Rather than relieving the problem the apostles are facing, Jesus expands it. He says to them, "Give them some food yourselves" (Mk 6:37).

Jesus is testing the apostles. Just as God tested the Israelites in the desert to see if they trusted him, now the Son of God tests his key followers out in a deserted place. Wilderness scenes are often settings of testing and trial in the scriptures. They are preparatory for whatever is next. If you feel like you are in the desert wilderness right now, God might be preparing you for what is to come.

The test of this gospel story is different from the one the Israelites experienced. Jesus tests the apostles to see if they have the same concern for the crowd that he has. Jesus has met the crowd's *spiritual* need to hear the Word of God. He now challenges the Twelve to see if they will tend to the crowd's *physical* needs. The challenge is whether they can find it within themselves to care about the crowd more than they care about themselves.

Growth is always at least somewhat difficult. God will intentionally make us uncomfortable to compel us to grow. We come to trust God when we are outside our comfort zone. And we grow to love and lead and care for others when we step outside our comfort zone too.

Jesus plans to hand on his movement that will be the Church to the apostles, but at this point they are immature. They have followed him because they want to be large and in charge. The gospels tell us they were constantly fighting over who would get to be the top guy next to Jesus once he established his kingdom. They wanted authority, power, and prestige; serving the needs of others was not on their agenda.

And so Jesus puts them in a position where they have to care for other people. He challenges them to look beyond themselves to the needs of others. He doesn't allow them to have the easy way out.

> **Tom:** Maybe as a parent this is where the Lord has you right now. You expect young children to be selfish, but when they remain that way into their teenage years, it's deeply disappointing. I have teenagers. Believe me, I know. They are facing challenges you and I never had. We wonder why they struggle in school or can't seem to make and maintain friends. You're concerned about their emotional health. But it's not just teenagers. At the parish, I talk to parents all the time who struggle in their relationships with their adult children too. They can be just as selfish and self-absorbed as teenagers. You just want the problem to go away, but Jesus wants you to grow as a more loving parent and sacrifice to meet the needs of your kids.

You might be frustrated at work as a team leader or manager. You have an employee who just doesn't seem competent. Maybe you have tried to move on from them, but God wants you to show servant leadership and coach the person up. God wants you to make an investment in them.

Maybe you're wondering if God is calling you to give more generously of your financial resources. The question becomes, are you using your money to bring blessing to other people or only for yourself? Perhaps you can feel that God wants you to give more resources to serve others.

Over and over again, God gives us opportunities to choose others' well-being over our own comfort. "For the Son of Man did not come to be served but to serve" (Mk 10:45). Comfort is good. We all like comfort. We like comfort food. We like to relax and get comfortable. We prefer comfortable shoes. We dress for comfort when we can. But comfort cannot be our guide and goal in life. Otherwise, it will get in the way of our calling.

Jesus did not use his privileged place for his own comfort; rather, he emptied himself to serve others. If we follow Jesus, he will lead us to the same place, where we have to choose between our comfort and service to others. That's what is going on with the disciples. Jesus, in his mercy, and as the strong leader he was, challenges the apostles to move beyond their comfort zone. He doesn't let them take the easy way out. But as we learn in the story, he doesn't leave them all alone in meeting the difficult challenge he places before them.

Jesus *tests* the apostles. He wants to see if they will take ownership of a problem that is not of their making. Will they step up and work toward a solution? And how well will they do? They respond, "Are we to buy two hundred days' wages worth of food and give it to them to eat?" (Mk 6:37). Their answer is a rebuke to Jesus: Are you crazy, Jesus? We can't do that. There is no way we can buy food for all these people. We don't have that kind of money. We don't have those resources. There is no place out here to even find such resources. You must be out of your mind.

So the apostles fail the first test. It's not that they give up because the task is too hard; it's that they don't even try. Rather than seek to solve the problem, they say it can't be done.

Since the apostles don't step up, Jesus coaches them up. He trains them to think differently. They are focused on what they lack. That can be a losing mindset unless you are also figuring out how to get the resources you need. Whenever we focus on what we don't have, using our lack as an excuse not to solve a problem, we put ourselves in a losing situation.

Jesus helps the apostles begin to see the situation another way. He asks, "How many loaves do you have? Go and see" (Mk 6:38). That is, before you come and tell me about what you *don't have*, go and see what you *do have*. Go take stock of what is around. By the way, it doesn't make sense to argue this miracle is about *sharing*, as some commentators have suggested. The apostles are given the task of taking stock of their provisions. If there had been enough to share, they would have found it. They didn't.

Jesus tells the apostles to find out what they have. This is so important for recognizing God's presence and power in our life. We have to know what we have, and what we lack, so that when God provides the miracle, we recognize it. God acts in our life all the time. To grow in faith, we have to be on the lookout for him.

Before we ask God for something, we have to acknowledge the gap we need God to fill.

- If you desire that God meet a financial need, calculate the need, and take stock of what you do have.
- If you lack time to accomplish everything you need to accomplish, determine how much time is currently at hand.
- If you feel a lack of emotional support, consider what support you already enjoy.

God provides for us so that we will see his power and presence in our lives. If you don't assess what you have, you won't recognize the miracle when it arrives. You won't see what God has done.

So the apostles proceed to assess what they have available. They come back with a report that they have five loaves and two fish—in other words, next to nothing. They probably related this information to Jesus with a "we told you so" attitude.

Jesus tells the apostles to arrange the people in groups: "So he gave orders to have them sit down in groups on the green grass. The people took their places in rows by hundreds and by fifties" (Mk 6:39–40). Miracles and management are not separate; in fact, they go together. Grace builds on nature. The way things work and the order in which they work are reflections of how God created the universe. God works through those systems even in miracles. Jesus has a method to manage this miracle: "Then, taking the five loaves and the two fish and looking up to heaven, he said the blessing, broke the loaves, and gave them to [his] disciples to set before the people; he also divided the two fish among them all" (Mk 6:41).

Jesus prays over the food, and then he gives it to the disciples. He wants them involved in the miracle from beginning to end. He wants them to be a part of it *and* to be perceived by the crowd as part of it. So, while they were not helpful in creating the plan, Jesus gets them to participate in three specific ways. They take stock of what they have, they arrange the people in rows, and they distribute the food. All three actions force the apostles to focus on the needs of others.

In a style that is typical to Mark's gospel, the results are understated: "They all ate and were satisfied" (Mk 6:42). They were not just satisfied physically. They were satisfied in their whole being; they were at peace. "And they picked up twelve wicker baskets full of fragments and what was left of the fish. Those who ate [of the loaves] were five thousand men" (Mk 6:43–44). Jesus sends the apostles out to collect the leftover food to feel the power of this miracle for themselves.

Why does God seem so uncooperative sometimes? Why does it seem like he thwarts us and actually gets in our way? He does it to help us grow. Only through obstacles does our trust in him increase. Only through obstacles do we grow out of our self-centeredness into servants: servant parents, servant friends, and servant Christ-followers.

REFLECTION QUESTIONS

1. What do you find yourself grumbling and complaining about most often?

2. What's the difference between complaining about God and complaining to God?

3. What problem are you currently facing or obstacle do you have to overcome? What step can you take that God might bless?

SERIOUSLY, PAIN IS A PROBLEM

Life is pain, highness. Anyone who says differently is selling something.

—Westley in *The Princess Bride*, by William Goldman

God whispers to us in our pleasures, speaks to us in our consciences, but shouts to us in our pain. It is God's megaphone to rouse a deaf world.

—*The Problem of Pain*, by C. S. Lewis

Father Michael: Kimberly was the indispensable person on our parish staff when Tom and I first came here. As is the case in many parishes with limited staffing, she filled a number of roles. But Kimberly took things to a whole different level.

Although her job title was director of faith for-
mation, she essentially served as office manager,
receptionist, sacristan, chief liturgist, chief of staff,
special events coordinator, and the list could probably go on and on.

In hindsight, all of that should have been a
big red flag, but I was a first-time pastor with no
experience in supervising a staff and little understanding of human nature. I was just grateful for
everything she did, considering how slender our
staffing and shallow our volunteer pool were. But
there was another thing about Kimberly. She was
always around. She had no family or friends outside the parish, no hobbies or interests beyond
her work, no life apart from her role at the church.
Only later would I learn that for years she had been
a virtual fixture at the rectory, evenings, weekends,
even holidays. More red flags.

What I did *not* know about Kimberly was that
she was an emotionally fragile person who was
very unhappy about my appointment as pastor.
Her unhappiness sprang from her fear that I would
threaten her hold on so much of parish life—which
unwittingly, but inevitably, I did. This unhappiness
and fragility were carefully kept from me under
a veneer of friendship and fulsome support for
everything we were doing. But eventually she
acted out in her pain with gossip. Complaining to
a growing circle of people, she spread increasingly

damaging falsehoods to strengthen the supposed legitimacy of her complaints.

To make a very long and sad story short, she more or less organized a coup, walking out at a most inconvenient moment and taking two other staff members with her. Her exit was undertaken in the most public manner possible, with a large circle of parishioners cc'd in her angry letter of resignation, leading to the angry departure of still others.

From beginning to end I handled the affair poorly. I failed to recognize the early warning signs and then turned a blind eye to the developing problems when they became obvious even to me. I had never in my life felt so exposed and betrayed. It was extremely painful and the most striking example in my experience of the maxim "Hurt people hurt people."

Pain presents a problem for Christians. No doubt about it. The classic argument goes like this: If God is all-good and all-powerful, then he will not allow pain and suffering. But since there *is* pain and suffering in the world, then God isn't all-good *or* God isn't all-powerful *or* God just doesn't care. It's as simple as that. And if it is that simple, then the case against Christianity is an open-and-shut one. At the same time, however, our dissatisfaction with pain and suffering offers a hint that we need a closer look at the topic.

In *The Problem of Pain*, C. S. Lewis writes that Christianity *creates* rather than *solves* the problem. Pain would hardly be a problem if we did not hope in an ultimate reality that is righteous and loving. The *problem* with pain is that we *have* a problem with pain—not just the physical fact of it but the disquiet in our minds, the heaviness of heart that the topic brings.

Pain is not a problem if there is not a loving God. If all of life came from chance or from a God who did not love us, we would accept pain and suffering the way fish accept water. We wouldn't question it. Yet we do. Something deep down in us knows that pain and suffering are not natural. They are at odds with how things are supposed to be.

That cry from our hearts points us toward a deeper understanding of reality. Our hearts can help us begin to see that the argument against Christianity is too narrow. It reduces our well-being simply to the absence of pain or just feeling good. If feeling good is the ultimate purpose of life, then a good God would not allow suffering. However, we know that feeling good is *not* the ultimate purpose of life. Any responsible parent knows this. They don't want their kids to suffer or be sad. But they know that children need to do things that don't feel good.

> **Tom:** It doesn't feel good to my kids when it comes time to eat dinner, brush their teeth, and go to bed. They resist it and fight me on it every night. However, I make them do it because I know that their bodily health depends on proper nutrition, good hygiene, and sufficient sleep.

Just as our bodies must experience some discomfort for our health and well-being, so must our hearts and souls. Scott Hahn writes, "God in his wisdom allows us to suffer." Now that doesn't sound very good. None of us likes suffering; we'll go to great lengths to avoid pain. But we understand that God allows it.

God does not cause or create suffering. He *allows* it. That's a subtle but important distinction to make. God is the uncaused cause of all that is good. He is the one who created the universe and everything in it. Ultimately, all good things come from him. Suffering and death were not caused by God. They came as a result of the Fall, following humanity's disobedience to God.

But while God did not intend for suffering and pain to happen, God *uses* them. Anyone can bring good out of good. God brings good out of evil. God uses pain for our good in *three ways*.

The *first way* we could call *disciplinary purposes*. Pain disciplines us so that we make better choices and decisions. It teaches us about how to live properly. For example, when you touch a hot stove, you feel pain and immediately pull your hand back. Without the pain, you would keep your hand on the stove and harm yourself further.

This is the way life works. Pain helps teach us about reality; it curbs our bad instincts and course-corrects us when we go in the wrong direction. Just as the pain of touching a hot stove teaches us about physical consequences, pain can teach us about spiritual and relational consequences too. When you lie and feel the pain of someone not trusting you afterward or feel the heartache of a broken relationship, the pain can teach you that lying just isn't worth it.

Our sins have necessary consequences. Sometimes our suffering comes as a result of sin: the ways we have missed the mark with our choices. God allows this suffering because he honors our choices and wants us to learn that sin is not worth it. The cost of sin is death.

This kind of suffering helps us to grow in character and opens us up to our need for God. In every sin, we put ourselves and our wants ahead of God and our relationship with him. Jesus shows this powerfully in the parable of the prodigal son (Lk 15:11–31). The son desires money and possessions over a good relationship with his father. The father allows him to make that choice. He respects his son's free will. The father lets the son make very bad decisions that leave him hungry and homeless, distressed and disgraced. Only when he is completely broken and literally starving to death does the son recognize his sin and how terrible life is apart from his father.

Pain teaches us about reality. It disciplines us to live in accordance with the fact that we are not the center of the universe. Pain can teach us that living for ourselves will not satisfy our hearts or souls in the end. We can understand this kind of suffering. We may not like it, but it makes sense.

Tom: The next two ways God uses pain for good take a little more explanation and can best be told by looking at two stories. The first is Father Michael's favorite Bible story.

JOSEPH'S FAVOR

The book of Genesis tells the story of creation, Adam and Eve, Noah and the Flood, the life and death of both Abraham and Isaac, and the adventures of Jacob. Then the action slows down to devote more than a dozen chapters to the story of one young man. With the exception of Jesus himself and a few others, the Bible tells us more about this guy than anyone in history. Who was he?

Jacob, son of Isaac, had twelve sons. Joseph was the eleventh born but his father's clear favorite. Joseph's brothers hated him for his position of favor. Of course Joseph did nothing but aggravate the situation. Although a person of good character with a big heart, he was a bit of a boaster. He apparently flaunted his fancy coat, which was the sign of his father's favor. And he could be a tattletale too. Then he makes a bad scenario worse by telling his brothers about his dream:

> He said to them, "Listen to this dream I had. There we were, binding sheaves in the field, when suddenly my sheaf rose to an upright position, and your sheaves formed a ring around my sheaf and bowed down to it." His brothers said to him, "Are you really going to make yourself king over us? Will you rule over us?" So they hated him all the more because of his dreams and his reports. (Gn 37:6–8)

Adding insult to injury, Joseph has a second dream along the same lines and again tells his brothers all about it. After the second time, even Joseph's father takes him aside and advises him to lay off sharing such self-aggrandizing stories. But it is too late. Joseph's brothers' hatred has become so inflamed that they openly discuss murder. At the last minute, one of them thinks better of this extreme action and convinces the others to sell Joseph into slavery instead—a pretty common occurrence at the time.

Joseph's brothers make up a story for their father. They take Joseph's fancy coat, smear it with blood, and report that Joseph was killed by a wild animal. Meanwhile Joseph is taken to Egypt. He is purchased by Potiphar, an official of the pharaoh's court. Potiphar is a person of wealth, influence, and power:

> The LORD was with Joseph and he enjoyed great success and was assigned to the household of his Egyptian master. When his master saw that the LORD was with him and brought him success in whatever he did, he favored Joseph and made him his personal attendant; he put him in charge of his household and entrusted to him all his possessions. (Gn 39:2–4)

Although Joseph is a slave, he is quickly given responsibility and authority over the household because of his obvious gifts and talents. Things go very well—for a while. But then trouble comes again for Joseph.

Turns out, Joseph is extremely handsome and unwittingly attracts the attention and romantic interest of Potiphar's wife. As a man of character, he resists her advances, which only incites her to become more aggressive, to no effect. Eventually feeling scorned, she accuses Joseph of the very unwelcome advances she was making. As a result,

"Joseph's master seized him and put him into the jail where the king's prisoners were confined. And there he sat, in jail. But the LORD was with Joseph" (Gn 39:20–21). Maybe by this point, Joseph was wishing the Lord was not "with him" so much; it didn't seem to help. So far he's been betrayed by his own brothers, sold into slavery, sexually harassed and falsely accused by his employers, and now unjustly imprisoned.

"But the LORD was with Joseph" (Gn 39:21). How exactly? "[He] showed him kindness by making the chief jailor well-disposed toward him. The chief jailor put Joseph in charge of all the prisoners in the jail" (Gn 39:21–22). Once again Joseph finds favor. That's really his story: favor. He enjoyed favor with his father, he had favor with Potiphar, and now he finds favor with the jailer, who essentially puts Joseph in charge of the prison.

In prison, Joseph meets the pharaoh's cupbearer and his baker, both imprisoned for some offense against the king. Each has a dream and shares it with Joseph who, being a dreamer, interprets it for them. He has good news for the cupbearer: in three days the pharaoh is going to restore him to his position. Bad news for the baker: in three days the pharaoh is going to impale him on a stake and vultures will dine on him. Ouch.

Joseph's interpretations of the dreams come to pass. The cupbearer is restored. But even though he had promised he would put in a good word for Joseph, he fails to do so. Joseph is betrayed once again.

Time passes. Joseph continues to languish in prison for a crime he didn't commit. Then one day, the pharaoh has a dream that agitates him. Its unsettling details must hold some important message, but none of his counselors can interpret what it might mean. The cupbearer remembers Joseph and his talent when it came to dreams, so the pharaoh sends for him. Joseph is willing to help but wants the pharaoh to understand that he can do nothing on his own: "'It is not I,' Joseph replied to Pharaoh, 'but God who will respond for the well-being of Pharaoh'" (Gn 41:16). In this moment, Joseph could have been tempted to boast about his abilities to earn favor with the king. Instead, he stays humble and introduces the pharaoh to the living God, assuring him of God's favor.

The pharaoh tells Joseph his dream. He saw seven fat, healthy cows and then seven anemic cows that emerged from the Nile and ate the healthy ones but remained thin and gaunt. Joseph explains the dream and what needs to be done. The next seven years will bring abundance but will be followed by seven years of famine. During the seven years of abundance, Joseph advises the pharaoh to appoint someone to prepare for the coming famine and keep the nation strong.

The pharaoh likes the idea and in an instant places Joseph in charge of the whole land. Joseph successfully undertakes the effort. As usual, he's up for the job. He organizes everything brilliantly and, in the process, becomes very wealthy and powerful because of his organization and leadership skills. Then, when the famine hits, Joseph manages the distribution of grains among the Egyptians as well as its sale to other countries, thereby amassing still greater wealth.

Two years into the famine, guess who comes knocking at the door looking for food? Guess who's actually bowing down to him now? Joseph's brothers. Only they don't recognize Joseph. He has grown of course, he is dressed in the Egyptian style, and he speaks to them in Egyptian, not their native Hebrew, so that his identity is perfectly concealed.

Joseph entertains his brothers, but he also tests them. He messes with them in part because he can and because that's what brothers do. But he also conceals his identity to see if they have had any change of heart. He wants to know if they have repented for the evil they did to him and have grown in wisdom. They prove themselves up to the challenge, demonstrating genuine humility in view of their circumstances and gratitude for Joseph's ability to save them. Speaking with them, Joseph becomes very distraught: "Joseph could no longer restrain himself in the presence of all his attendants, so he cried out, 'Have everyone withdraw from me!' So no one attended him when he made himself known to his brothers. But his sobs were so loud that the Egyptians heard him, and so the news reached Pharaoh's house" (Gn 45:1–2).

After about twenty years of separation from his family, Joseph experiences a flood of emotion. As his brothers stand before him, he no doubt feels all the pain of the betrayal and injustice he had suffered at their hands and those of others. That happens sometimes. You hear a name from the past or a song on the radio, you come across an old photo or cross paths with a former friend, and suddenly you're thrown into a world of hurt you thought was behind you. You can't control it.

Joseph sobs as he remembers the villainy of his brothers. Then he gets hold of his emotions and reveals his identity: "'I am Joseph,' he said to his brothers. 'Is my father still alive?' But his brothers could give him no answer, so dumbfounded were they at him. 'Come closer to me,' Joseph told his brothers. When they had done so, he said: 'I am your brother Joseph, whom you sold into Egypt" (Gn 45:3–4).

The brothers can't believe it. They are astonished and afraid. Would he seek retribution for their betrayal? Instead, Joseph shares an incredible insight into pain and suffering. He says, "But now do not be distressed, and do not be angry with yourselves for having sold me here. It was really for the sake of saving lives that God sent me here ahead of you" (Gn 45:5).

Joseph can look back at the suffering in his life without bitterness, recognizing God's hand. He understands that *God* had really sent him to Egypt. God had been at work all along. Because Joseph sees this clearly, he can comfort his brothers and help them overcome their guilt and fear. God used Joseph's pain to save lives. If Joseph had not been there to interpret the pharaoh's dream, the years of abundance and plenty would have been wasted, and the years of famine would have been devastating.

Joseph tells his brothers that the famine will continue for another five years. Then he says, "God, therefore, sent

me on ahead of you to ensure for you a remnant on earth
and to save your lives in an extraordinary deliverance. So it
was not really you but God who had me come here; and he
has made me a father to Pharaoh, lord of all his household,
and ruler over the whole land of Egypt" (Gn 45:7–8).

This is the key lesson from the long story of Joseph. God
can use our pain and suffering for the good of *others*. Moth-
ers know this intuitively. They must bear the discomfort of
carrying a child for nine months. Then they suffer through
childbirth. Fathers may suffer to watch their wives in pain,
but it is hardly comparable.

> **Tom:** My wife, Mia, has given birth eight times. Of
> course she never looks forward to the pain but
> after the birth of every one of our children, the
> suffering is nothing to her in comparison to the
> miracle of our new child. She knows it has led to
> something beautiful. The greatest joy I have ever
> witnessed is the joy my wife experiences when
> she sees our new baby for the first time.

The *second way* that God uses our pain is for *the good of
others*. This important insight appears again at the end of
Joseph's story, which is also the end of the book of Genesis. The brothers fear that Joseph will take revenge on them
after all: "Now that their father was dead, Joseph's brothers became fearful and thought, 'Suppose Joseph has been
nursing a grudge against us and now most certainly will pay
us back in full for all the wrong we did him!'" (Gn 50:15).

If you have seen the Godfather movies, you know that in *Godfather II*, Michael Corleone learns that his brother Fredo betrayed him: "I know it was you, Fredo, you broke my heart. You broke my heart." He decides he will have his revenge but not until his mother passes so she doesn't have to mourn the death of her son. Well, that is exactly what Joseph's brothers fear. They fear that since their father has died, Joseph will have his revenge. They believe that Joseph may have been harboring a grudge over all those years.

> So they sent to Joseph and said: "Before your father died, he gave us these instructions: 'Thus you shall say to Joseph: Please forgive the criminal wrongdoing of your brothers, who treated you harmfully.' So now please forgive the crime that we, the servants of the God of your father, committed." When they said this to him, Joseph broke into tears. Then his brothers also proceeded to fling themselves down before him and said, "We are your slaves!" (Gn 50:16–18)

The brothers throw themselves down and ask for Joseph's mercy. But Joseph had no evil intent. He replies, "Do not fear. Can I take the place of God? Even though you meant harm to me, God meant it for good, to achieve this present end, the survival of many people" (Gn 50:19–20).

Throughout his life, Joseph experienced suffering at the hands of others. They used their free will to do him harm rather than good. He suffered because of his brothers' jealousy, as well as the infidelity and dishonesty of Potiphar's wife. He suffered because of the baker's ingratitude. People meant to harm him, but he never allowed the harm inflicted by others to change his perspective on God. He could see that when people wanted to harm him, God could bring good out of it. God's intentions for him were always good.

At this point, it could be argued, *Well, Joseph can say that now. Everything worked out for him. He had power and possessions and popularity.* But Joseph showed his belief in that truth throughout his experience. In every instance, he applied his talents to the opportunities he was given. God was with him, and he acted like God was with him.

Even when you experience pain because others treat you poorly, do not allow that to change your attitude toward God. God intends good. God intends to bring good out of evil. If you stay focused on God's goodness and do not get bitter, God will use your pain for the benefit of others, just as he did with Joseph.

PAUL'S PROBLEM

Another story in scripture perfectly illustrates our point. The story takes place in the Acts of the Apostles. Written by the evangelist Luke and serving as a sequel to his gospel, Acts tells the story of the first followers of Jesus, which we noted in chapter 3. It recounts how the Church gained momentum and members in the ancient world after Jesus' resurrection. Most of the book focuses on Peter and Paul and their influence in various places of the ancient Roman Empire. Peter is the focus of the first half of the book, and Paul becomes the central figure of the second half.

At a certain point, Paul and his coworker Barnabas are commissioned by the early Christians to go out into the world to share the Good News of the Gospel with the non-Jewish community. Until this point, most Christians were Jews who followed Jewish customs and law. Paul and Barnabas were sent beyond the Jewish community—to the Gentiles and pagans who worshipped Greek and Roman gods.

Paul made numerous missionary journeys, extended trips for the purpose of evangelization. He took these trips for the same reason you might travel for business— to grow and strengthen your organization—only he did it for Christianity. Paul was a pioneer, expanding the reach and influence of Christianity ever wider. But he was also an entrepreneur planting new church communities and helping them go deeper in their faith.

This story takes place at the end of Paul's first missionary journey. Although Paul has been on this trip for a couple of years, he hasn't gotten very far afield, no more than several hundred miles. In the first century, travel was slow and difficult. When Paul got to a destination, he settled in to spend some time getting to know the community and making his case for Christ. Here's what happens at the end of this first trip: "At Lystra there was a crippled man, lame from birth, who had never walked. He listened to Paul speaking, who looked intently at him, saw that he had the faith to be healed, and called out in a loud voice, 'Stand up straight on your feet.' He jumped up and began to walk about" (Acts 14:8–10).

Lystra was in the Roman province of Galatia, in modern-day Turkey. Paul is giving a speech about Jesus.

As he speaks, Paul scans the crowd and sees a man paying close attention (as a speaker, it's always encouraging to
know that at least one person is listening to you). By the
power of the Holy Spirit, Paul senses that this man, who has
never walked, has faith to be healed. So Paul yells out for the
man to stand up and walk. He does so immediately.

Paul was an educated man, a scholar of the Law. He
knew the Old Testament inside and out. He could debate
the Pharisees and hold his own with Greek philosophers.
But he also was a faith healer. He performed miracles and
healed people by God's power throughout his ministry.
Reason and faith in miracles are not mutually exclusive.

The story continues: "When the crowds saw what Paul
had done, they cried out in Lycaonian, 'The gods have come
down to us in human form.' They called Barnabas 'Zeus'
and Paul 'Hermes'" (Acts 14:11–12). Paul heals this guy to
inspire faith in God, but the healing effects the opposite of
his intention. The pagan crowds recognize the healing, but
rather than attributing it to Jesus the Christ, they assume
they are in the presence of their own deities. They proclaim
Paul and Barnabas gods.

Ever been mistaken for a god before? Neither have we.
But all of us know the uncomfortable feeling of being mistaken for someone or something we are not. Worse still is
when our intentions are misunderstood. So Paul and Barnabas have to deal with this gross misunderstanding. Then
the situation gets even worse: "And the priest of Zeus,
whose temple was at the entrance to the city, brought oxen

and garlands to the gates, for he together with the people intended to offer sacrifice" (Acts 14:13).

In pagan culture, one honored the gods by making animal sacrifices to them. It was the accepted offering, just as we might make a financial offering at Mass. The temple priest prepares to make just such a sacrificial offering to Paul and Barnabas, much to their horror. For a good Jew like Paul, idolatry was the very worst sin, and this was taking it to a whole new level. They know they have to stop these proceedings, bring order to the scene, and correct the misunderstanding of the crowd.

> The apostles Barnabas and Paul tore their garments when they heard this and rushed out into the crowd, shouting, "Men, why are you doing this? We are of the same nature as you, human beings. We proclaim to you good news that you should turn from these idols to the living God, 'who made heaven and earth and sea and all that is in them.'" . . . Even with these words, they scarcely restrained the crowds from offering sacrifice to them. (Acts 14:14–15, 18)

They manage to slow the crowd down and clearly express their message of the truth of the living Lord. But things grow still worse: "However, some Jews from Antioch and Iconium arrived and won over the crowds. They stoned Paul and dragged him out of the city, supposing that he was dead" (Acts 14:19). Luke does not offer much detail here. One minute the crowds want to worship Paul as a god, and the next minute they seek to stone him to death. What happens in between these two scenes?

When crowds come together, it creates a certain kind of energy, positive or negative. People gathered at sporting events often feed off one another and work themselves into agitated enthusiasm, even frenzy. A political rally that generates anger can escalate into a riot. A religious revival can become overwhelmingly emotional. The energy must have an expression and an outlet. That is what is happening here. The crowd has seen something amazing, and when they cannot express their amazement in worship, it needs some place to go. Jewish leaders who regularly cause trouble for Paul (just as they had for Jesus) seize that moment to turn the crowd against him. Perhaps they suggest to the crowd that if these men weren't gods and they had miraculous powers, they must be malevolent forces.

In any event the crowd turns ugly. They drag Paul's apparently lifeless body outside of the town, supposing he is dead.

> But when the disciples gathered around him, he got up and entered the city. On the following day he left with Barnabas for Derbe. After they had proclaimed the good news to that city and made a considerable number of disciples, they returned to Lystra and to Iconium and to Antioch. (Acts 14:20–21)

Again, Luke does not offer much detail. The disciples must have given Paul medical treatment and prayed for his healing. Maybe he was not as badly injured as it appeared. But Paul is one tough guy, and he gets up and walks to another town called Derbe. And Derbe was not around the block. It was sixty miles from Lystra. So Paul is quickly and apparently wholly healed and confidently goes on to the next town to teach and preach.

Derbe is the last new place they visit. They then retrace their steps to the towns previously visited, working their way back to the city of Antioch, where their journey began. The Acts of the Apostles continues: "They strengthened the spirits of the disciples and exhorted them to persevere in the faith" (Acts 14:22).

Father Michael: Wait! Stop right there!

Paul exhorts and encourages the disciples to *persevere in the faith*? If you were having a cup of coffee with him (or a glass of wine—Paul was a wine drinker), you might say, "Are you crazy? Paul, look what your faith got you! Out of obedience to God, you traveled to all these towns telling people about Jesus. You traveled at a time when travel was brutally difficult; you had to walk for miles between towns. All your teaching and preaching seems to have landed on deaf ears. And your good deeds nearly get you killed. Your God seems to be OK with that. In fact, he sent you into that situation. So, Paul, it does not make sense to *persevere in the faith*."

Paul would maybe look at you and smile. Perhaps he might say, "I know all that. Those are facts. But here is something else I have learned. Facts can obscure deeper truths." When you get too focused on facts and don't look at the bigger picture, fact is the enemy of truth. Here is the deeper truth he came to believe: "It is necessary for us to undergo many hardships to enter the kingdom of God" (Acts 14:22).

That's the good news! It might not sound like it on the surface. No one wants to go through hardships, but they prepare us and make us grow so that we can experience the greater rewards of God's kingdom. This is good news because it means that your struggles and your suffering are worthwhile. Your pain has a purpose.

That's the *third way* God uses pain for our good—*to help us grow and mature to live in the place of perfect joy that is heaven.* You have heard the saying "You can't get there from here." Well, you can't get to heaven without some sort of pain. We all go through many hardships in this life. When you endure difficulties and still believe in God's goodness and love, you are growing into a person who truly loves God. When you go through trials and hold on to hope in God's goodness, you are becoming someone who can breathe the air of heaven. The path of pain can purify us, perfecting us for the life of heaven.

Think about it this way. Have you ever wondered why we call them "the pearly gates"? In every old joke about heaven, St. Peter stands guard in front of the so-called pearly gates. The reference actually comes from scripture: "The twelve gates were twelve pearls, each of the gates made from a single pearl" (Rv 21:21).

Think for a moment. How is pearl formed? Through irritation. A granule of sand gets inside an oyster shell and irritates the oyster. So, it forms a protective covering around the granule that hardens into a smooth pearl. In the irritation, the oyster creates something beautiful. In our hardships and struggles, even in our irritations, God wants to do something beautiful in us. He wants to form us into beautiful souls. Our role is to persevere in faith, no matter what pain and suffering life may bring our way. God will work within our pain to bring goodness in one way or another. Through many hardships we enter into heaven. But more awaits us there. "We know that all things work for good for those who love God, who are called according to his purpose" (Rom 8:28). Do you know what "all things" means in the original Greek? We're no Greek scholars, but we think it means "all things."

God can use every pain and all suffering to bring about our good. When we are suffering, when our heart is hurting, it is very difficult for us to think that God can use it all. We just want it to go away. But stop and think for a second: What if it is true? What if God really *can* use all your pain and suffering? Doesn't that change everything? Doesn't that change everything about the pain your loved ones have endured? It means all our pain and suffering can have meaning.

When we experience pain and suffering we often ask, *Why?*

- *Why is this happening?*
- *Why did you allow it?*
- *Why aren't you doing anything, God?*

Asking why is natural, but it's the wrong question in the midst of suffering. We have both asked it in times of trouble, but for pain to serve a purpose, we must change our question from *Why?* to *What?*

Instead of asking, *Why is this happening?* we should ask God,

- *What do you want to do in the midst of this pain?*
- *What work are you doing in me?*
- *What do you want me to do and to become?*

All things will eventually work together for our good. We will see some of that worked out in this life on earth just as Joseph did. Joseph could look back at the end of his life and see how God had made his life work out. Certainly, we should have our eyes open for that and believe that God might be using our hardships to bring about a good we will experience on this earth. At the same time, we know that doesn't always happen. Some stories seem to end in tragedy. Some relationships are never reconciled. Some losses seem permanent or in no way retrievable on this earth. But faith tells us it only *seems* so.

Here's the promise of heaven: our pain and suffering will be redeemed. God is taking the worst failures, the most difficult times of your life, and is shaping them into something beautiful for you in heaven. Does that sound too good to be true? On earth we say that if it sounds too good to be true, it probably is. That's because we live in a fallen world. But when we're talking about heaven, then it *must* be true. When our hearts are longing for something and wish it to be true, it touches on the eternity our hearts hold. In that moment, we have begun to see the truth of heaven. Pain perfects us so we can enjoy the perfect place that is heaven.

God uses our pain to teach us how to live properly. God uses our pain to benefit others. God uses our pain to perfect us.

REFLECTION QUESTIONS

1.   Why is pain only a problem if there is a good and loving God?

2.   What good might God want to bring out of the pain you have endured from other people's decisions?

3.   Do you believe God can use your suffering to do something beautiful in your life? Why or why not?

SERIOUSLY, WHY DID HE HAVE TO DIE?

The cords of death encompassed me;
the torrents of destruction terrified me.

—Psalm 18:5

Do not go gentle into that good night.
Rage, rage against the dying of the light.

—Dylan Thomas,
"Do Not Go Gentle into That Good Night"

Rob Belanger pretty much had it all: movie-star good looks, an electric smile, a winning personality. You couldn't help but like him. More than that, though, he was a salt-of-the-earth kind of guy. A dedicated husband and father to his two girls, he coached their teams and invested in all his players. He was a thoughtful neighbor and great friend.

His coworkers at a very prestigious financial firm in downtown Baltimore liked him and highly valued his work.

Though an accomplished musician, Rob waited humbly and patiently in the pews until we recognized his ability and invited him to step up and start serving. And he did, serving our parish for years with dedication, passion, and purpose. We have had many talented musicians on our team over the years, but Rob was more. Rob wasn't just a *music* leader; he was a *worship* leader, leading others into worship through music. At the same time, he had a drive for excellence that pushed other musicians to give their best while inspiring the congregation.

When we found out Rob had cancer, we prayed he would beat it. Our whole church prayed for him. We prayed hard, in a consistent and dedicated way. Some on staff fasted too. Rob went through every kind of treatment available at the world-class health-care facilities right here in Baltimore. He traveled elsewhere for experimental treatments as well. At one point it looked like a miracle cure would save him, but it was not to be. Rob succumbed to the cancer at Christmas in 2016. It seemed a cruel twist that Rob died during a season when he usually would have been leading thousands in the celebration of the Nativity.

Father Michael: My first question when I get to heaven is, "What the heck were you thinking when it came to Rob?" Rob's death just didn't make sense. He was a force for good in his family, the community, and the Church. Surely God could have intervened in some way. Why allow Rob to

die, and why allow the suffering his loss caused to
his family and friends? It didn't make sense that
God wouldn't heal him.

No matter who you are, this topic probably hits you in some
personal way. Maybe you know someone who suffered
through a debilitating disease and then died. Or maybe it
wasn't the suffering part but the loss part; you lost someone
to an accidental death or a sudden one, and you struggle
to understand why they were taken so quickly. If you were
God, you wouldn't have taken them that way. They had so
much unfinished business, such obvious potential for good
things. It seems especially painful when someone making a
contribution to others dies in their prime. The loss can be
staggering.

Why, God, did you let that happen? we inevitably ask.
And sometimes the answers that Christians offer really don't
help. They sound trite or out of touch with reality, or just
plain condescending. At Rob's funeral, one well-meaning
parishioner remarked, "God took Rob because he wanted
him in the heavenly choir." Still deep in mourning and dis-
belief, all we could think was, *Ugh! Please, for the love of
God, be quiet. You are not helping!*

While all of us will die, not all deaths are in God's tim-
ing or according to his will. Some people do die before God
wants them to die. Violent death through war or terrorism
and death as a consequence of reckless or dangerous behavior are not part of God's plan. Victims of physical and mental illness are not part of God's plan. Deaths from murder
and abortion stand in stark opposition to God's plan. God's

will is opposed in our world all the time. Remember, don't confuse *life* not making sense with *God* not making sense.

THE ROAD TO THE CROSS

Here's a thought that you might not have considered—Jesus' death didn't make sense in many of these very ways. He suffered greatly in the course of his crucifixion and died a violent, tragic death that left his friends and followers bewildered and broken.

And here's the thing: it was all so unexpected, so untimely, so shocking. He was in the prime of his life. Here was a guy who had crowds of people following him. They marveled at his teaching and flocked to hear his preaching. His popularity and political savvy allowed him to challenge the status quo. The religious and political leaders of the day constantly tried to trip him up and trap him, but Jesus outmaneuvered and outwitted them. The whole trajectory of his public life was unmistakably headed toward increasing power and authority.

That's why the apostles followed him. It's hard to believe that they signed on to his team for purely altruistic or religious reasons. They likely didn't follow Jesus because it was the right thing to do—they followed Jesus because his star was on the rise. The disciples just wanted to ride his coattails. When Jesus finally got to the top, they wanted to be there with him. They wanted to share in the power and glory that would come when Jesus was large and in charge.

Jesus too wanted power and glory. However, he understood that the route to power and glory would be different than what the disciples expected. It is different from what the world expects. So one day he took his closest friends on a little journey to give them some insight: "After six days Jesus took Peter, James, and John his brother, and led them up a high mountain by themselves" (Mt 17:1). Well, six days after what? Six days earlier, Jesus took the apostles to a place called Caesarea Philippi and asked them an important question: "Who do you say that I am?" (Mt 16:15). Peter responds that Jesus is the Messiah; he is the Son of God. Jesus tells Peter that he is absolutely correct, and on this faith, his faith, the Church would be built. After that, Jesus reveals to the apostles that as the Messiah, he must go to Jerusalem, suffer at the hands of the religious leaders, be nailed to a cross, and then rise from the dead. He teaches them that if anyone wants to follow him, they have to pick up their own cross, thus suggesting the type of death they will be required to suffer.

Coming on the heels of all these alarming and unexpected announcements, this trip up the mountain results in an amazing sight: "And he was transfigured before them; his face shone like the sun and his clothes became white as light" (Mt 17:2). Up on the mountain, Jesus is transfigured. His face and clothes shine bright as light. He no longer looks like an ordinary man because his divinity is revealed, if only for a moment. Jesus is 100 percent God and 100 percent man. As he walked this earth, his divinity was hidden. However, in this moment, Jesus lets Peter, James, and John see the truth of his divine nature. They get a glimpse of Jesus' glory.

And behold, Moses and Elijah appeared to them, conversing with him. Then Peter said to Jesus in reply, "Lord, it is good that we are here. If you wish, I will make three tents here, one for you, one for Moses, and one for Elijah." (Mt 17:3–4)

Peter proposes remaining on the mountain. No more trooping around working to get people on board and win them over. Why not set up camp, stay awhile, and let everyone come and experience this amazing scene too? All the talk of crosses, suffering, and death fades in the dazzling scene that is unfolding.

The experience is so wonderful that Peter just wants it to last, to keep going. And this is only natural. When you have a mountaintop experience as Peter, James, and John had, you want to extend it. You don't want it to end. Whether your experience is a concert, a conference, or some kind of celebration centered on you, perhaps graduation or your wedding day, you just don't want it to end.

Mountaintop experiences are important when it comes to our faith. Everyone needs them. We have had our own such experiences when we felt God's presence and power. Hearing Pope John Paul II at World Youth Day preach "Be not afraid!" to a cheering crowd of on-fire young people was a memorable mountaintop experience. Going to Saddleback Church for the first time and finding a community of people engaged in their faith was an incredible mountaintop experience. Closing our church building one Christmas Eve and hosting a communitywide celebration *out in* the community *for* the community was a life-changing mountaintop experience.

If you have never had a mountaintop experience, we hope you do sometime soon. God gives them to us to strengthen our faith. In fact, that's what Jesus is doing here. He knows that his coming suffering and death will shake the faith of Peter and the others. So Jesus exposes his closest friends to this experience to strengthen them.

Jesus wants to give Peter a mountaintop experience *for a moment*, but it can't last in this world. This life is a pilgrimage; at no point in it do we reach our destination. And for each one of us, that pilgrimage, that journey, must eventually lead to the Cross.

Dazzled by the experience, Peter impulsively makes this suggestion about setting up tents. In a way, he is tempting Jesus from his own journey to the Cross, although he doesn't realize it. Peter fails to grasp that once again he is opposing God. The thought of not saying anything doesn't occur to Peter. And so God the Father speaks up: "While [Peter] was still speaking, behold, a bright cloud cast a shadow over them, then from the cloud came a voice that said, 'This is my beloved Son, with whom I am well pleased; listen to him'" (Mt 17:5). As Peter is talking, God the Father interrupts him, which is ironic because Peter is always interrupting everybody else and speaking out of turn. The Father affirms that Jesus is his beloved Son to whom they should be listening. Specifically, they should listen to him as he describes his suffering and death as an integral part of his mission.

As we see over and over again in the gospels, whenever Jesus connects his mission as the Messiah with his suffering and death, the apostles tune him out. It doesn't square with their view in which the Messiah isn't supposed to suffer and die. The chosen one, as they understand it, is supposed to rally the people of Israel, lead them into battle, destroy their Roman oppressors, and establish Israel as an independent nation under God's rule. If Jesus was the Messiah, any talk of his suffering and death didn't make sense with this scenario.

The voice of the Father tells the apostles to pay attention to Jesus when they would rather have ignored him. But the disciples probably didn't catch much of the meaning: "When the disciples heard this, they fell prostrate and were very much afraid. But Jesus came and touched them, saying, 'Rise, and do not be afraid.' And when the disciples raised their eyes, they saw no one else but Jesus alone" (Mt 17:6–8). As quickly as they experienced Jesus in his glory, he was back to his normal appearance. One moment the apostles hear the voice of the Father and witness the glory of God, and in the next moment, it is gone. We can have some experiences with God that are so clear and overwhelming and then, in a moment, they are gone. But they are real and unmistakable.

As they are coming down the mountain, Jesus commands them, "Do not tell the vision to anyone until the Son of Man has been raised from the dead" (Mt 17:9). Jesus tells the apostles to keep quiet about what they have seen—the bright light, the cloud, Elijah and Moses, the voice, all of it—until his resurrection. The apostles, of course, don't understand why their silence is necessary. But he is trying to control events until his time is complete and he has accomplished his mission.

After Jesus was crucified, died, and was buried, none of the apostles waited outside the tomb for him to rise from the dead. They thought it was all over—game, set, match. They counted their hopes dashed, their dreams dead. They were wrong and Jesus wasn't who they thought he was. He was a great preacher and teacher, maybe even a prophet, but he definitely wasn't the long-awaited Messiah. They could not comprehend the connection between Jesus' suffering and death and his future glory.

The Transfiguration, which is what this event is called, is intended to show us the connection between Christ's humiliation and suffering on the Cross and his glory. It foreshadows both the Passion and the Resurrection. It was intended to help both the apostles and us to see that the suffering Jesus endured on the Cross, while an apparent failure, is actually his greatest victory.

The Transfiguration parallels the Passion in many striking ways. At the Transfiguration, the experience is glorious; at the Crucifixion, the experience is agonizing. In both cases, Jesus climbs a mountain. In both cases, Jesus invites Peter, James, and John to pray with him. In both cases, he is lifted up between two men. At the Transfiguration, he is between two great men, Moses and Elijah; at the Crucifixion, he is between two criminals.

At the Transfiguration, all is light, while at the Crucifixion, darkness descends on the earth. At the Transfiguration, Jesus' clothes become dazzling white, while on the Cross, he is stripped of his garments. The Transfiguration shows Jesus' hidden glory, while during the Passion he is publicly humiliated.

But in both experiences he is exalted because he is obedient, obedient even to death on the Cross. Suffering and death are not the end of the story; they're just the introduction to the Resurrection. And what is true for Jesus in this regard is true for us.

Although we cannot provide an explanation for every human experience, the Cross offers us hope that God can take any suffering, any death, and bring about good from it. He used the suffering and death of his Son to redeem the whole world. It stands to reason that he can take the suffering and death of the people you and I love and use them for great good too.

Why did God allow Rob to die? Why did he allow your loved one to die? We don't know the answer with 100 percent certainty, but for Christians the Cross seems to hold the answers. When we look at the Cross, we know that people don't die because God doesn't love us. We know the answer cannot be that God didn't love Rob. Remembering the Cross, we know the answer is not that we are not loved. It can't be that God doesn't care. God takes our suffering so seriously that he took it upon himself on the Cross, and the Father accepted Jesus' loving sacrifice to redeem all human suffering.

In Jesus' life, the agony of the Cross, the reality of human suffering, and the damage of sin are inseparably bound to the glory of the Resurrection. And they can be in our experience too.

When we lose a loved one, we tend to focus on our *loss*, which of course is natural and important. Grieving is crucial to healing. But it is also true that we too often look at what we have lost to the neglect of considering what our loved one has gained. If a loved one has gone to the Cross with Jesus and joined their suffering to his, then they have entered into the Father's glory. God allows good people to die because God wants them to share in the glory of heaven. That is the end for which we are made and the ultimate reward to which we strive in our lives as disciples of the Lord Jesus. Dying is not the end for us. We are intended to live in the glory of heaven.

In his letter to the Philippians, Paul writes,

> Have among yourselves the same attitude that is also yours in Christ Jesus, who, though he was in the form of God, did not regard equality with God something to be grasped. Rather, he emptied himself, taking the form of a slave, coming in human likeness, and found human in appearance, he humbled himself, becoming obedient to death, even death on a cross. Because of this, God greatly exalted him and bestowed on him the name that is above every name, that at the name of Jesus every knee should bend, of those in heaven and on earth and under the earth, and every tongue confess that Jesus Christ is Lord, to the glory of God the Father. (Phil 2:5–11)

Anyone who knew Rob and witnessed how he handled his impending death would see that he didn't lose his battle with cancer. Through the whole experience he never faltered or failed in his faith. He had fears, he had tears. There were dark days and long, sleepless nights. But he held on to hope and trusted in God every step of the way. He believed in God's goodness until the end. That example for friends and family alike was powerful and purposeful. It touched and changed many hearts.

There was more than grace in this experience; there was "glory." While his death was certainly a huge loss to us and our community, in the end Rob won.

THE ROAD TO EMMAUS

While it can be comforting to know that friends and family members who have died have gone on to light and life in the Lord, we must still shoulder the burden of living without them. This brings the risk of losing our grasp on hope or at least forming doubts about the future. Our hope for the future is often tied to our relationships with other people, and when they're gone, we can be confused about where we are and where we are going. That was true for Jesus' followers after his death, as we learn from Luke's gospel: "Now that very day two of them were going to a village seven miles from Jerusalem called Emmaus, and they were conversing about all the things that had occurred" (Lk 24:13–14).

Here we meet two of Jesus' disciples within just a couple of days after he was crucified. Jesus had just twelve apostles, his closest associates, but he had many more disciples, or students who faithfully followed him, at least until his arrest and crucifixion. After his death, most of them dispersed out of fear or confusion. These two were leaving Jerusalem and taking the seven-mile hike to a town called Emmaus, a journey that would have taken about two hours on foot.

Luke tells us that the two were "conversing about all the things that had occurred." Doubtless they were discussing the amazing and horrifying week that had just passed. First, Jesus triumphantly entered Jerusalem to the cheers of the crowds and celebration in the city. And then, just days later, he suffered a total fall from grace in a humiliating death.

The two disciples are walking away from the other disciples because Jesus is dead. As far as they can see, his death meant an end to the movement he had started and the future it held. Like all of his disciples, they had followed Jesus because they believed he would improve their lives and change the course of history. Now, there was nothing left for them in Jerusalem. Additionally, it was dangerous to associate with other followers of Jesus. They have to look for a positive future somewhere else. Interestingly, they are walking west, into the sunset, at the close of day, which adds an element of melancholy to the tale. It is getting darker and darker.

This can reflect our story too. When a loved one dies, we feel like life is getting darker. Hope seems elusive. You may have had hopes for the future with a spouse, a child, a friend, or a business partner. Their death means not only the end of a relationship but the end of our dreams and plans for a bright future with them.

Like the disciples, in moments like these we need to discuss the loss. We need to talk about it. Conversations with people who care can help us make some sense of it all. We have a fundamental need to express our grief, to be heard and understood. We naturally look for people who can identify with our thoughts and fears, our concerns and confusion.

Luke continues: "And it happened that while they were conversing and debating, Jesus himself drew near and walked with them, but their eyes were prevented from recognizing him" (24:15–16). As they are walking and talking, Jesus approaches, but they don't recognize him. Perhaps this was because the risen Lord looked so completely transformed, or maybe this detail simply reveals the utter darkness of their minds. They were talking about Jesus, but they couldn't even recognize him when he was right next to them. Often in the midst of grief or loss, it can be incredibly difficult to see God even if he is walking with us. Grief can lead to darkness, to blindness.

Now, Jesus could have revealed himself to them right away, showing them he was alive. But he didn't. He walks with them instead. He doesn't just give them answers right away. He lets them try to figure it out for themselves for a while. We each must do exactly the same in times of loss and grief. These disciples were probably talking in circles, poring over the events again and again—gaining no insights, drawing no conclusions. It was basically a confused conversation between two confused people. Then, Luke says, "He asked them, 'What are you discussing as you walk along?' They stopped, looking downcast" (24:17).

Ever ask a question, and accidentally, you hit a pain point? It stops someone in their tracks. Accidentally, you hit a pain point. You didn't know it was a pain point, but you ask a perfectly innocent question and clearly you hit a nerve. It stops someone completely. That's what happens here. And if you are grieving the loss of someone, maybe that's happening to you *often*. The smallest thing anyone says that reminds you of a loved one can be overwhelming.

Luke continues: "One of them, named Cleopas, said to him in reply, 'Are you the only visitor to Jerusalem who does not know of the things that have taken place there in these days?'" (24:18). Cleopas is basically saying, Where have you been? Don't you know what just happened? It would be like someone asking in 2020, "What is COVID-19?" There likely wasn't a lot of other news out there. Everyone was talking about the events of the past week. The whole community was discussing Jesus' triumph, his arrest, his trial, and his execution.

"And he replied to them, 'What sort of things?'" (Lk 24:19). This question holds incredible irony. The two disciples are talking about Jesus, and they don't even know he's walking with them. Jesus must have had to force himself not to smile. But he wasn't just playing with them, he was engaging them.

Tom: Michael and I wrote a book titled *Rebuilt*, which tells the story and shares the strategies God used to turn our parish around. The book sold

quite well in Catholic churchworld. One time, I was
away at a men's retreat in Colorado. On the first
morning, at breakfast, I struck up a conversation
with a fellow retreatant about books we were currently reading. We shared titles and comments
with growing excitement as we came to realize
how much we had in common, bookwise. At one
point he turned to me and said enthusiastically,
"Hey, have you ever read *Rebuilt*?" For a few minutes I allowed him to comment on it, because I
wanted to hear what he would honestly say (for-
tunately, he was quite positive about it). But eventually I could not keep up the pretense—I have no
poker face. Coyly I smiled and said, "Yea, actually I
kind of wrote it."

The disciples were talking about Jesus and the events that
happened to *him*. But cleverly he asks the disciples what sort
of things had happened to *them*. He gives them an opportunity to express themselves. If you are disappointed with God
and feeling frustrated and confused, then go ahead and yell
at him. The psalmists yelled at God all the time. For example, in Psalm 13, David says, "How long, LORD? Will you
utterly forget me?" (v. 2). That is, any day now, Lord. Any
day you feel like showing up and helping me out, I'll take
it. On the Cross, Jesus quoted another psalm: "My God, my
God, why have you abandoned me?" (Ps 22:2).

Jesus wants to hear from you. What's happened to you?
What have you lost? How does that make you feel? Angry,
lonely, sad, mad, confused? Talk to him and tell him.

It doesn't even have to be a lot. Just say from your heart: "Jesus, I am lonely. Jesus, I am confused. Jesus, I am angry. Jesus, I am worried." Those little thoughts open the door to a broader conversation with him. He will listen to you just as he invited the disciples he met on the road to Emmaus to share what was on their hearts.

> They said to him, "The things that happened to Jesus, the Nazarene, who was a prophet mighty in deed and word before God and all the people, how our chief priests and rulers both handed him over to a sentence of death and crucified him." (Lk 24:19–20)

Cleopas says that they were talking about Jesus of Nazareth. He describes him as "mighty" in both word and deed. Maybe you have never thought about Jesus in that way. Often the pictures of Jesus in religious pop culture make him look soft and weak. He is the "Buddy Christ," affecting a silly smile, who just wants to be friends. Perhaps you have those images of Jesus in mind and that's why you have never thought of following him. Quite honestly, we wouldn't follow him either if we thought those images reflected Jesus' personality and character.

The real Jesus is not simply a nice guy. The real Jesus is powerful. He is mighty. Crowds of people followed him because they experienced his power. They felt the power of his personality and the strength of his character. They knew that he spoke with authority—that his words were not empty clichés but truth he lived out personally.

Cleopas had followed Jesus because he was a leader worth following. This disciple's disappointment echoes in perhaps the saddest line in the story: "But we were hoping that he would be the one to redeem Israel" (Lk 24:21). *We were hoping.* It sounds so wistful, almost forlorn. Other translations say, *We had hoped.* They had stopped hoping; they had lost hope. "We had hoped" are words of dejection. Not only have things gone poorly but the months they spent with Jesus now seem a waste of time. These are the words of people who have lost not only their leader but also their future. Their hope is dead. They could have been looking for a better life somewhere else.

In his book *All Things New*, John Eldredge notes that there are three different degrees of hope. The first is *casual hope.* I hope it doesn't rain tonight. I hope my garden grows this spring. Casual hopes are good things we desire that bring pleasure and satisfaction into our lives. When we lose out on casual hopes, we suffer some disappointment. We might be in a bad mood for a little while, but we move on and get over it pretty quickly. Casual hopes are small and often point to or support a deeper level of hope.

The second degree of hope is *precious hope.* These are hopes for the major areas of our lives. You hope to have a joyful and life-giving marriage. You hope to run a successful business that can feed your family and make a positive impact in your community. You hope to see your children's children.

Our precious hopes are far more valuable than our casual hopes. When they are disappointed, it comes as a serious setback. When they are dashed, it is heartbreaking. Healing, if it is to come, requires grace—and time. While the loss of precious hopes can devastate us, it does not have to crush our spirit completely. We can rebound because there is a third degree of hope.

Our *ultimate hope* is that on which we rest our souls, our very selves. Your ultimate hope is what you ultimately believe will bring blessing and purpose into your life. Ultimate hope is what you trust to make things work out in the end.

There really is only one truth in all of human history that is big enough to support your ultimate hope. If we place our ultimate hope on anything else, we set ourselves up for disappointment and disillusionment. This is what Cleopas and the other disciple had done. They were hoping that Israel would be redeemed. Everyone knew that Israel needed to be redeemed. The nation and the people had lost their way. They were supposed to be a light to the nations but instead were just a dusty outpost of the Roman Empire. God had promised that the whole world would be blessed through the nation of Israel, but instead the Israelites had become so insular, self-centered, and weak that they couldn't bless anyone, not even themselves. So, many of the Israelites hoped that God would redeem them by sending a Messiah who would overthrow the power of the Roman Empire and set up a political kingdom. But God had a bigger plan.

Jesus begins to share God's bigger plan: "And he said to them, 'Oh, how foolish you are! How slow of heart to believe all the prophets spoke! Was it not necessary that the Messiah should suffer these things and enter into his glory?' Then beginning with Moses and all the prophets, he interpreted to them what referred to him in all the scriptures'" (Lk 24:25–27).

Jesus corrects them. He explains that their hopes were muddled and misguided. What you thought had dashed your hope—the death of Jesus—was actually necessary for your hope to be fulfilled. You were hoping that Israel would be redeemed. You thought of the redemption as a political insurrection. Your hope was too *small.* You were putting hope in something that was much smaller than God's plans.

In order to redeem Israel, the Messiah had to suffer and die, and so enter his glory. There is that word again: *glory.* The Messiah entered into his glory by his death. But the glory was not just for the Messiah; it was for the whole nation of Israel. And with the Messiah entering into his glory, Israel *would become* a light to the nations. The whole world would be blessed by Israel through the death and resurrection of the Suffering Servant referred to in the prophets. God's plan all along had been to send his Son into the world to die for the world. Their hoping had to be adjusted to God's bigger plan.

You might be thinking, *What does that have to do with me and my loss?* When we experience a loss, we tend to focus on *what* we lost or *who* we lost. It is only natural. The hurt in our heart feels all-encompassing as if it is the only reality. But if we can, at least eventually, pull back and look past our loss to see that death is not the end. Jesus' resurrection meant the renewal and restoration of the whole world. It meant that everything had changed for everyone.

Does this mean you and I should not grieve the loss of loved ones? No, of course not. Grief is good. Grief is needed. Grief is a necessary part of the process after the loss of anything in life. But it is *part* of the process, not a final destination. Especially when it comes to death. Death doesn't have the final word. Resurrection does.

The apostle Paul, who had seen the resurrected Jesus, went so far as to mock death. Death had been conquered by Jesus. And so he says, "Death is swallowed up in victory. Where, O death, is your victory? Where, O death, is your sting?" (1 Cor 15:54–55).

As the disciples walk with the Lord, they eventually come to see that Jesus' death had not been the end. The Resurrection had been part of his plan all along. They come to understand how God took the greatest evil and turned it into the greatest good.

The story continues: "As they approached the village to which they were going, he gave the impression that he was going on farther. But they urged him, 'Stay with us, for it is nearly evening and the day is almost over.' So he went in to stay with them" (Lk 24:28–29). The disciples still believe that they are speaking to a stranger. Freed from their focus on self, the two begin to turn outward. Inviting him to dine with them is a sign of the fellowship and intimacy that have quickly developed. Cleopas and his friend move from their own sadness to a willingness to care for someone else. And this prepares them to recognize God's presence.

> And it happened that, while he was with them at table, he took bread, said the blessing, broke it, and gave it to

them. With that their eyes were opened and they recognized him, but he vanished from their sight. (Lk
24:30–31)

In the breaking of the bread, their eyes are opened and they
recognize Jesus. This is the "real presence" of the eucharistic
Lord who has been traveling with them all along: "Then they
said to each other, 'Were not our hearts burning [within us]
while he spoke to us on the way and opened the scriptures
to us?'" (Lk 24:32).

When Jesus broke open the scriptures to them, he put
the story of what God was doing in a larger context. The
burning of their hearts within them signals that their hope
was being restored. So much so that they run back to Jerusalem to tell others what they have experienced, what they
now know: Jesus is not dead but risen from the dead. He is
alive.

The two disciples discovered that the one in whom they
had placed their hope was among the living. This is our
hope as well when we lose a loved one—we rightly cling to
the belief that they are among the living. We have lost them
for a time, but not forever.

Father Michael: Good friends of ours, Al and
Abby, lost their twenty-one-year-old son, Isaac.
He was riding a bicycle when he was hit by a car
and instantly killed. By all accounts he was an
exceptional young man: a great athlete; serious
scholar, with a special interest in philosophy and
theology; and a prodigious artist, who had already
developed a very original and attractive style of

painting. But most of all, he was a young man of deep and growing faith who surely would have had a positive, perhaps even powerful, impact on the Christian community, maybe a vocation to the priesthood.

Tom: At the viewing for his son, I went up to Al and tried to think of something, anything, to say. Having a son about the same age, I couldn't imagine where he was at emotionally. I wanted to say something that spoke to Al's heart. But words failed me. All I could say was, "Al, I'm sorry. I do not know what to say." The grief of the moment in that room overwhelmed me. Then I greeted his wife, Abby, with the same helpless words. Hoping to say something more profound, again all I could muster was "I'm sorry." And then she said, "It isn't supposed to end like this." Without thinking I responded, "It isn't the end." Quite honestly, I don't know If that remark comforted her or offended her. But I meant it; I believe it. And if the unthinkable ever happened to me, I pray I could hold on to this truth.

It's not right for any parent to bury their child. It's not the way it's supposed to end. But it is not the end. Death does not have the final say. Jesus' resurrection tells us that death is *not* the end. Death is a door to something more. It is the door to our ultimate hope, which is in heaven. Our ultimate hope is in the Resurrection.

REFLECTION QUESTIONS

1. Whose death have you struggled to make sense of because it seemed so unfair?

2. Have you had the experience of someone dying well as Rob did? What *glory* did their death reveal?

3. How does hope in the Resurrection change our attitude toward death?

Conclusion

THE MIDDLE OF A LARGER STORY

Good movies create tension by building interest in charac-
ters and the events of their lives. They capture and hold our
interest with unresolved questions and twists and turns of
the plot. We keep watching because we want to know how
it all works out.

But did you ever tune in to a movie halfway through?
You're interested, but it's difficult to follow. There are char-
acters you don't know, relationships you don't understand,
and plot developments you can't quite follow. You've missed
too much of the story to make sense of it all.

In many ways that describes our lives. Life is a drama. It
is why dramatic movies appeal to us—they are a reflection
of our lives; our lives are stories. But we are in the middle
of those stories. And of course there is one big difference
between our lives and the movies. We know how the story
ends because God has revealed the ending for us in the

143

scriptures. While we cannot know all the details, by reading the scriptures and walking with others in faith, we come to better understand our place in God's plan.

Throughout this book, we have shared with you Bible stories that we hope help you better understand your story within God's story. The stories of Joseph and Jonah and all the rest can help us see that the questions we confront, and the struggles in which we find ourselves, have been faced by people in every generation. Those stories of real people and real encounters with God give us a clearer perspective on our own lives.

Good movies, good novels, and good stories have good endings; they bring everything together in the end. They tie together the pieces that didn't make sense when they were introduced or stood unresolved in the narrative. The same is true for our stories. They *will* end well; everything will be brought to resolution if we follow the Lord and seek always to grow in understanding how he acts in our lives, our stories.

We want to share with you the end of our story. It is the end that God wills for every single person he has ever created. We find the end of the story in the very last book of the Bible, the book of Revelation.

Perhaps no other book of the Bible needs more explanation than Revelation. It gets quoted or referenced in disaster movies and popular culture all the time. Think of your favorite disaster movie and probably there is some reference to Revelation. Its dark images and fantastical scenes lend themselves well to the genre, though such references probably contribute to misunderstanding about it.

The book of Revelation can also be difficult because it is full of figurative language and rich symbolism in numbers, colors, and landscapes. Another reason the book can be hard to appreciate is that the story does not advance in a linear manner. Rather, the narrative unfolds in circular repetitions that can be hard to follow (think of the movie *Pulp Fiction*).

But here's the point: there is an inner logic to the book of Revelation. Its elaborate structure reveals an incredible genius and depth of knowledge. The book is called Revelation because it reveals the risen Jesus' knowledge of what must and will happen in history and at the end of history. Jesus allows the author John to see these events from the perspective of heaven, and what will happen at the end of the world.

If you were to ask most people what happens to this world in the end, they would say it will be destroyed. Many Christians believe that at the apocalypse, God will completely annihilate the earth and the good people will escape the coming destruction and go to heaven. That's what they think *and* they're completely wrong. That's *not* what happens. Here's the real end of the story. After God has defeated all evil and corruption: "Then I saw a new heaven and a new earth. The former heaven and the former earth had passed away, and the sea was no more" (Rv 21:1). After the battle of good and evil is complete, John sees a new heaven and a new earth. The world as we now know it is gone, but at the same time it is still earth. John recognizes it as the earth renewed and restored. If someone promised you a new car with lots of fancy new features, you would certainly recognize it as new. But you would also easily recognize that it was a car.

> **Tom:** A couple of years ago, I went to visit a parish in San Francisco. The pastor, Father Roger, took me out to dinner at a nice restaurant. To make the experience all the more fun, he borrowed a friend's Tesla sedan. I had never seen a Tesla up close before. The car had incredible features. After dinner, he showed me one of them. The car could be programmed to blink its lights and open doors and windows in sync to music. He played "Carol of the Bells," and it was amazing to watch. People in the parking lot gathered around to see the show.

As cool as the Tesla is, it is still just a car. It still has four tires and a steering wheel. I could tell it was a car. John, who sees this vision of the future, recognizes the earth because he sees that it *is* the earth—only now it is new and restored.

Neither of us is much into fantasy literature or science fiction. Quite honestly, we have never understood the huge hype about *Star Wars*. We know that's heresy to some of you, and maybe you're now ready to discount everything else we've said in this book. But hold on one second. While we have never understood the enthusiasm for fantasy entertainment, there is something we have learned to appreciate.

The genre itself points to the ache in our hearts for heaven and eternity. In all those books, movies, and video games, there is a whole new world, but it isn't *entirely* new. We recognize the world, but there is something fantastic, wonderful, and frightening about it. The reason those books and movies speak to us is because there will be a new earth that will be our home. G. K. Chesterton wrote about this blend of the familiar and the new, "to be at once astonished at the world and yet at home in it."

Many popular images of heaven paint a portrait of a place very different from the world we know, with lots of fluffy white clouds and annoying harp music. But consistently, scripture describes heaven in terms very familiar to us: roads and buildings, gates and doors, water and fire. Could it be that heaven will be recognizable to us in many ways? Could it be that our experience of this world, in many ways, is preparatory for what will come?

John sees a new heaven and a new earth. His vision continues: "I also saw the holy city, a new Jerusalem, coming down out of heaven from God, prepared as a bride adorned for her husband" (Rv 21:2). The city of Jerusalem represents all of the earth. At the end of time there is a marriage of heaven and earth; they are brought together. The earth is not obliterated; it is *joined* to heaven. God loves the world and his creation, and so his desire and will are for complete unity.

Perhaps the last chapter of the Bible sounds like a fairy tale in which the prince rescues and weds the maiden in distress, and they live happily ever after. Those fairy tales are faint anticipations and foreshadowing of the true story that is God's plan for his beloved, the human race.

John sees a new Jerusalem. John loved Jerusalem. Our cities and towns mean something to us, don't they? We both love Philadelphia because we have deep roots there. We both love Baltimore, especially north Baltimore, because it is our adopted hometown. It's important that we appreciate our hometowns, communities, and neighborhoods, but that doesn't mean we turn a blind to its many problems and challenges.

Jesus loved Jerusalem. Jesus wept over Jerusalem too. He was keenly aware of the city's many faults and flaws. John sees a Jerusalem restored and renewed, looking beautiful, like a bride on her wedding day. Pious Jews pray for this daily, and John says that it is coming. The future in heaven is the restoration of all the things you love. Heaven is the renewal of all things you love. The renewal of all things simply means that the earth you love—all the special places and treasured memories you have—are restored.

John's vision continues: "I heard a loud voice from the throne saying, 'Behold, God's dwelling is with the human race. He will dwell with them and they will be his people and God himself will always be with them [as their God]. He will wipe every tear from their eyes, and there shall be no more death or mourning, wailing or pain, [for] the old order has passed away'" (Rv 21:3–4).

God will dwell with us. He will be with us, present to us completely and totally. We will feel his presence and know his power. In this world, we struggle to know God's presence at times, maybe much of the time. It is sometimes difficult to maintain a lively awareness that God is with us and for us. The world, the flesh, and the devil detract from God's presence. We drift. We are prone to wander, liable to leave the Lord out of the picture. In the marriage of the new heaven and the new earth, we will have such an intimacy with God that we will be keenly aware of his presence all the time. We will be without sin, so we will desire and want his presence always.

Revelation says God will wipe away every tear from our eyes. There will be no more crying, no more death, no more mourning or pain because all of those things are part of the fallen world, and they will pass away. There is no crying in baseball, and there is no crying in heaven. But here's the thing: When John says there will be no more crying, he doesn't just mean that there will no longer be things to make us sad but that even the past hurts will pass away. They will cease to exist. In the words of J. R. R. Tolkien's Samwise Gamgee, "Everything sad [is] going to come untrue."

Isn't that a beautiful idea? That not only will there be no future crying or pain or death but all of the pain we have undergone will come untrue, that the wounds and hurt from our past will be so completely healed that it will be as if it had never happened. Think of the regrets you have from the past, think of the broken relationships, think of your failures and things you wish you had done differently. All will cease to exist.

You may be thinking that just sounds like wishful thinking, too good to be true. Let us repeat a thought from chapter 5. On earth if we say something sounds too good to be true, *it probably is*. But in the new heaven and the new earth, if something sounds too good to be true, it *must* be true. It is part of the ache for eternity that has been put on our hearts. "The one who sat on the throne said, 'Behold, I make all things new.' Then he said, 'Write these words down, for they are trustworthy and true'" (Rv 21:5).

> **Father Michael:** That Christmas Rob died, I visited him in the hospital as much as I could. My visit the day after Christmas was an especially difficult one. It was clear he was failing, and the family was heartbroken and exhausted. I went home that evening with a heavy heart. I couldn't sleep that night and ended up on my sofa sitting in the dark. Eventually I drifted off and suddenly found myself in what was the clearest, most realistic dream I have ever had. I was still sitting on my sofa and Rob was standing between me and the front door. He said, "I'm leaving now." And I said, "Rob, don't go, I don't want you to go."
>
> He said, "It's time, I have to go." And with that, he opened the door and started to step out, only to turn back, his face transformed. He said, "They're beautiful, they're so beautiful." "Who?" I asked. "Who are you talking about?" As he stepped out the door, he simply said, "The angels."
>
> The exchange was so remarkably real, so chilling, I woke out of my deep sleep, wide awake and certain of every detail of the dream. Quickly I decided to return to the hospital. It was only when I arrived that I learned Rob had just died.

We are both quite sure that dream came from God, who makes all things new. Live in the hope of that promise and always keep in mind, "Everything sad [is] going to come untrue."

IN MEMORIAM

Christopher and Isaac,
beloved sons.

Connor,
Michael's assistant and friend.

Donald,
Tom's dad.

Rob,
an inspiration to us both.

May God's light and life shine upon you
until we meet again in the coming kingdom.

REFERENCES AND RESOURCES

Alcorn, Randy. *Everything You Always Wanted to Know about Heaven*. Carol Stream, IL: Tyndale House, 2014.

Cavins, Jeff. *When You Suffer: Biblical Keys for Hope and Understanding*. Cincinnati, OH: Franciscan Media, 2015.

Chesterton, G. K. *The G. K. Chesterton Collection*. London: Catholic Way Publishing, 2012.

Eldredge, John. *All Things New: Heaven, Earth, and the Restoration of Everything You Love*. Nashville, TN: Nelson Books, 2017.

Hahn, Scott. *A Father Who Keeps His Promises: God's Covenant Love in Scripture*. Cincinnati, OH: Servant Press, 1989.

John Paul II. *Be Not Afraid: Pope John Paul II's Words of Faith, Hope, and Love*. Philadelphia: Running Press, 2006.

Keller, Timothy. *Jesus the King: Understanding the Life and Death of the Son of God*. New York: Penguin Group, 2011.

———. *Making Sense of God: An Invitation to the Skeptical.* New York: Penguin Books, 2018.

———. *Walking with God through Pain and Suffering.* New York: Riverhead Books, 2013.

Kreeft, Peter. *Heaven: The Heart's Deepest Longing.* San Francisco: Harper and Row Publishers, 1980.

———. *Three Philosophies of Life.* San Francisco: Ignatius Press, 1989.

———. *You Can Understand the Bible.* Ann Arbor, MI: Servant Publications, 1990.

Lewis, C. S. *Mere Christianity.* New York: HarperOne, 2015.

———. *The Problem of Pain.* New York: HarperOne, 2015.

———. *The Weight of Glory.* New York: HarperOne, 2001.

Martin, James. *Jesus: A Pilgrimage.* New York: HarperCollins, 2014.

Sheen, Fulton. *The Life of Christ.* New York: Doubleday, 1958.

Stanley, Andy. *The Grace of God.* Nashville, TN: Thomas Nelson, 2010.

Willard, Dallas. *The Divine Conspiracy: Rediscovering Our Hidden Life in God.* New York: HarperCollins, 1998.

Williamson, Peter. *Revelation.* Grand Rapids, MI: Baker Publishing, 2015.

Wright, N. T. *Simply Christian: Why Christianity Makes Sense.* New York: HarperCollins, 2006.

———. *Surprised by Hope.* New York: HarperCollins, 2008.

Yancey, Philip. *Disappointment with God: Three Questions No One Asks Aloud.* Grand Rapids, MI: Zondervan, 2009.

REBUILT RESOURCES

Church of the Nativity
20 East Ridgely Road, Timonium, MD
ChurchNativity.com.
Nativity Online: www.churchnativity.com/nativity-online/
Facebook: facebook.com/churchnativity
Rev. Michael White
Twitter (Fr. Michael): @nativitypastor
Make Church Matter (blog): nativitypastor.tv

Rebuilt
Rebuilt Parish Association: rebuiltparish.com

Rebuilt Parish Podcast: rebuiltparish.podbean.com

Rebuilt Books
White, Michael, and Tom Corcoran. *ChurchMoney: Rebuilding the Way We Fund Our Mission.* Notre Dame, IN: Ave Maria Press, 2019.

———. *Rebuilding Your Message: Practical Tools to Strengthen Your Preaching and Teaching.* Notre Dame, IN: Ave Maria Press, 2015.

———. *Rebuilt: Awakening the Faithful, Reaching the Lost, Making Church Matter.* Notre Dame, IN: Ave Maria Press, 2013.

———. *The Rebuilt Field Guide: Ten Steps for Getting Started.* Notre Dame, IN: Ave Maria Press, 2016.

———. *Tools for Rebuilding: 75 Really, Really Practical Ways to Make Your Parish Better.* Notre Dame, IN: Ave Maria Press, 2013.

Fr. Michael White and **Tom Corcoran** are the award-winning and bestselling coauthors of *Rebuilt, Tools for Rebuilding, Rebuilding Your Message,* and *ChurchMoney,* as well as the bestselling Messages series for Advent and Lent.

During their time at Church of the Nativity in Timonium, Maryland, the parish has tripled in weekend attendance while developing a strong online presence, reaching thousands more people each week. The growth of the parish also is evident in increased giving and service.

Since the publication of *Rebuilt,* White and Corcoran have spoken at national and international conferences and regularly appeared on Catholic radio and television, including EWTN and CatholicTV. Together they launched the Rebuilt Parish Association, directly helping other parishes with their renewal efforts.

Corcoran is the pastoral associate at Church of the Nativity. He completed undergraduate studies at Loyola University Maryland and graduate studies in theology at Franciscan University of Steubenville.

White, the pastor of Church of the Nativity, earned a bachelor's degree from Loyola University Maryland and graduate degrees in sacred theology and ecclesiology from the Pontifical Gregorian University in Rome. He served as priest-secretary to the archbishop of Baltimore and directed the papal visit of Pope John Paul II to Baltimore.

churchnativity.com
rebuiltparish.com
rebuiltparish.podbean.com
Facebook: churchnativity
Twitter: @churchnativity
Instagram: @churchnativity

Read *Seriously, God?* with your book club, small group, or parish!

FREE resources and videos are available for discussion, prayer, and reflection.

Visit **avemariapress.com/seriously-god** to find:
- leader's guide
- companion videos
- small-group discussion questions
- downloadable posters, flyers, and digital graphics
- and more!

ALSO BY MICHAEL WHITE AND TOM COCORAN

Look for these titles wherever books and eBooks are sold.